BOOKS BY LOU TABORY

Inshore Fly Fishing

Lou Tabory's Guide to
Saltwater Baits and Their Imitations

Lou Tabory's Guide to Saltwater Baits and Their Imitations

LOU TABORY'S
GUIDE TO

SALTWATER BAITS AND THEIR IMITATIONS

LOU TABORY

Foreword by John Merwin
Illustrations by Dann Jacobus

Lyons & Burford, Publishers

TO MY WIFE BARB—
MY FAVORITE FISHING PARTNER

10 9 8 7 6 5 4 3 2 1

Printed in Hong Kong

Design by Cindy LaBreacht

Tabory, Lou
    [Guide to saltwater baits & their imitations]
    Lou Tabory's guide to saltwater baits & their imitations / Lou Tabory ; illustrations by Dann Jacobus.
p. cm.
    Inlcudes bibliographical references (p.) and index.
    ISBN 1-55821-361-9 (paper-over-board)
    1. Saltwater fly fishing 2. Flies, Artificial. 3. Baitfish.
I. Title. II. Title: Guide to saltwater baits & their imitations.
SH456.2.T32 1995
799.1'6—dc20   95-6011
                                                  CIP

C O N T E N T S

ACKNOWLEDGMENTS

*S*pecial thanks and gratitude to

TOM HALAVIK, for the many hours of putting together pages of information that would have taken me years to compile. It helped to have a professional wade through the mountains of data and give me the meat. And to the United States Department of the Interior Fish and Wildlife Service for their help and for having talented people like Tom on their staff.

ANGUS CAMERON, whose counsel and supervision made the contents of this book so much better, and for the wonderful hours we have spent together talking fishing.

DANN JACOBUS, whose remarkable artistic talents make this book come to life, and for being so easy to work with.

And thanks also to
RICHARD STOLL, who took the time to write a nine-page letter on northern Pacific baits, their reactions, and the reactions of gamefish to them. I was enlightened and amused to learn that 3,000 miles across the country salmon feed much like our stripers do. Your information on the Puget Sound, and the surrounding areas, was priceless. Thanks.

Putnam Photo of Danbury, CT—for all the help and sound advice on the photos in this book.

Larry Kennedy—an old friend and fine guide, who gave me such good insights on baits and fishing along the southern Atlantic coast.

Allen Frens, and Captain Frank Catino—for their insights on southern and shallow-water fishing.

Steve Huff and Rick Ruoff—through our casual talks I learned much about flats fishing.

Steve Hein and the State of Louisiana Department of Wildlife and Fisheries—for sound and complete information about the important baits of the Gulf of Mexico.

Rod MacLeod and the State of Connecticut Department of Environmental Protection—for the information on baits in Long Island Sound.

Dave Beshara, Eric Peterson, Bill Peabody, and Dennis Goddard—all master fly tyers who helped with fly patterns and fly design.

Dan Blanton, Nick Curcione, and Bob Popovics—longtime friends whose knowledge about baits in their respective locations and help with fly patterns was invaluable.

Dave Hayward—for insights and knowledge on fly types and baits along the Gulf of Mexico.

John Posh—for help in gathering baits and keen insight about fishing.

Pip Winslow—for input on baits in the large estuaries of northern Massachusetts.

I'm sure I have missed people who helped with information for the book, and I know I did not include many friends who have shared their knowledge with me over the years—to all, many thanks.

FOREWORD

*M*y friend Dick wears a back brace when he fly fishes for striped bass; he says it helps him through long hours of casting. But one night near Sandy Hook, New Jersey, as I listened to him jingle and clank his way along a quiet beach, I decided it was because of all the gear he carries. Every gadget known to anglers is loaded in his assorted hip-, chest-, and backpacks where multiple layers of fly boxes strain the zippers: a mushroom cloud of equipment supported in distant profile by thin stems of legs that struggle in the waves.

He finds some security in this, I suppose. The ocean is a big place and standing at the edge of it with fly rod in hand may be the ultimate lesson in humility. And for that reason, being dressed like a giant Swiss army knife can be reassuring. By virtue of long experience, skilled casting, and sometimes a little luck my friend catches more than his share of stripers. All of his other gear not withstanding, he does this—like everybody else—with one fly at a time. It is on that fly, that one simple bit of feathers and fur, that success or failure ultimately rides.

After all the mechanics of tackle, casting, and water-reading skills are mastered, choosing the right fly is the essential question. It's the basic element in fly fishing, whether the target is brown trout or bonefish, striped bass or steelhead. Because no single fly pattern works all of the time for any particular fish, the fly-pattern possibilities have become both legion and often bewildering.

Historically, fishermen have partly solved the fly-selection problem by matching the hatch, generally imitating with a particular fly whatever the fish happen to be eating at a particular moment. As natural fish foods change from hour to hour, day to day, and place to place, fly patterns are changed likewise. Over several centuries of trout fishing, this has come to mean tens of thousands of different trout-fly patterns more or less matching hundreds of different insects. Fly pattern choices have consequently become less random but no less difficult. The knowledge required to pull one successful hatch-matching pattern from a box of several hundred choices can be enormous.

It is this difficulty that accounts for the wide popularity of generally representative trout flies like the Adams or Grey Fox Variant, flies that are sufficiently imitative to work often and widely, while not being exactly so. And it is the same fishing problem that accounts for the wide popularity of angling writers such as Art Flick and Lou Tabory, men who have been able to simplify the whole business, thereby bringing effective fly fishing within easy reach of more people.

Flick's small and basic *Streamside Guide* has for many years been the user-friendly bible for trout fishermen wanting to get just far enough into hatch-matching to catch a few fish but not so far in as to be swamped with detail. He was as friendly and matter-of-fact in person as he was in print, teaching us when to use a Grey Fox Variant and why, and when to switch to an olive in a few short, easy pages.

Tabory approaches the same basic questions in salt water with the same easy manner. Here's what you need to know, and no more than that. Stand here. Tie on this fly. Cast over there. And that's all there is to it.

I have been privileged—and lucky—to have fished with Lou Tabory off and on for almost twenty years. He is without question one of the most exceptionally skilled anglers I've met anywhere. One proof of that pudding has come often when we've packed or unloaded a truck full of tackle in the course of a trip to the Massachusetts coast or Connecticut shore. After everything's set up and organized, what actually goes in the fishing bag is one fly box. Rarely two, and never more than that. Just a few flies tooled with years of experience. A box to kill for.

The answers to most of my questions over the years have been in that box, which I've raided freely and often. And those same answers are in this book, which will make your saltwater fly-fishing life both more simple and more productive. Read it, and then throw your back-brace away.

—JOHN MERWIN
Dorset, Vermont

INTRODUCTION

$\mathcal{S}$electing the right fly pattern baffles the average saltwater fly angler as much as it once did the trout fisherman. Many anglers simply want to go fishing, tie on a fly, and catch some fish. Though the serious angler, the researcher, enjoys studying the foods that fish eat, most saltwater fly rodders want a few flies that they can use with confidence, not two dozen different patterns in the fly box to worry about. Choosing the proper fly during a mayfly hatch is often simple. You see the fly on the surface, then match it with one of similar size, shape, and color from your fly box. If you don't have the right pattern, you still *know* the fly you need. The problem in salt water is seeing the foods, which are not as obvious as a mayfly, unless you know where to look and what to look for. Finding the baits that fish are feeding on not only helps you with fly selection, it also helps find the fish. Time spent learning the foods and their imitations will certainly increase an angler's success in salt water; it will also increase an angler's pleasure. To some this is a part of fly-fishing tradition; trout anglers often delight in knowing the Latin names and life cycles of insects. Surely this makes them better anglers. But do you need to learn the food's Latin name to catch fish? No, nor should you need to count fins or check mouth shapes to identify a species of saltwater baitfish.

This book is meant to offer help, advice, and information to saltwater fly rodders at all levels. It will give the serious researcher a place to start digging, and the beginner or more casual angler, a simple list of flies that work in many locations for many species of fish; the serious and expert angler should gain fresh insights into saltwater baits. This book will simplify and categorize the important foods of saltwater gamefish, by putting the baits into like groups. It should help the marine fly rodder realize, for instance, that a striper fly will catch many other species, and that a fly pattern should be classified by the baits it represents rather than by the species of fish it is intended to catch.

After thumbing through several fly pattern books, I realize how bewildering saltwater fly patterns can be to many anglers. The fly rodder sees bluefish flies that look like trout flies, and trout flies that catch weakfish. In one book alone there are nearly 500 saltwater patterns, with over 70 tarpon flies; yet in the sea there are only about a dozen important families of baits. Within these families there are perhaps three dozen species that are significant, and some of these baits, or their young, look alike. Knowledgeable anglers enjoy experimenting with different types and styles of flies, and for those people who like tinkering with new patterns, I can only say: Keep developing more creations!

But many fly rodders need some guidance. They need to know the important baits and what fly types effectively imitate them. They need to have several good fly patterns that will catch fish in a particular area, without stocking a gunny sack of flies. This book will give the novice some guidelines, a place to start learning the best fly type and size for a certain location. It will also help the traveling angler with fly selection, as well as the experienced angler who wants to learn more about the different foods that saltwater fish eat. For years, freshwater anglers have studied the trout's diet, learned the mayfly's life cycle, and become better fishermen. This can also be true for the saltwater fly angler. Saltwater gamefish need to search for food constantly; unlike river trout, which live right in the grocery store, saltwater species must find locations with food. The fly rodder who knows these locations, which foods will be found there, and how to imitate them, will catch more fish.

Luckily, saltwater baits are less complex than freshwater aquatic insects. There are literally thousands of species and subspecies of foods, but in a certain location there are usually only a few important foods. And there are many similar foods that do not require special treatment. Some foods in the sea fall into groups of like appearance. And it is often possible to match several different baits with a single fly pattern and color. For example: Set side by side a three-inch silversides, an anchovy, a sardine, and a herring, and you will see that they are similar in appearance. Saltwater baits generally hatch, grow to adult size, and live in specific locations throughout the season. Many develop in estuaries. This book will cover where and when baits spawn, how they grow, where they might be located at a given time of the year, and how they act in the water. Knowing the spawning times of big baits is important in some areas, because the angler can thereby determine the approximate arrival time of the young. The spawning times of small foods is insignificant unless spawning brings the adults into a certain location in good numbers, providing easy feeding for gamefish.

While researching saltwater baits for *Inshore Fly Fishing*, I realized that a more detailed text, a saltwater seaside guide, would help anglers become more knowledgeable. As I studied, I found a wealth of information that has improved my own fishing. This guide is not a scientific textbook. There will be no *"Stenonema vicarium"* references, other than to identify the species. I still refer to a certain type of mayfly as an olive #20 that floats. I know the basics of aquatic insects, but not the

Latin names. My goal here is to teach the angler to identify a bait by general size, shape, and color, without counting fin rays or scales. Then I'll match that bait with a fly pattern. If a type of bait has a number of different lookalike species in its family, as does the silversides, I'll discuss all as one food type. I will mention only the more important species. Some families have over 100 subspecies. And just because one of these subspecies might be common in a small creek in Turkeybeak, Georgia, that doesn't make it a substantial food source in the Atlantic. Since most subspecies are identical to major species, there is no reason to mention them. Only if a certain species within a group is special will I mention it, and even then only if its behavior is significant enough to make its mention important to the angler.

Along with the major bait types, juvenile gamefish are fair game for the adults. Like trout and black bass, marine predators consume their own young, or the young of other gamefish. The savage baby bluefish, while feeding on baits, may itself become dinner for a bigger fish. (See section on juvenile gamefish.)

Some major foods will receive less attention because their size makes them too large to copy realistically with a fly. Except in billfishing, which requires only a few short casts with an oversize fly, bulky flies are difficult to cast. Realistically, seven- to eight-inch patterns are all that most fly rodders can handle. Some oversize foods reach a length of eighteen inches. In such cases I will discuss mainly the juveniles of the species, for they are the most significant to the fly rodder. Yes, there are some oversize patterns that a few anglers use; however, most fly rodders will suffer when trying to cast these feather dusters. In the wind, even an expert caster will struggle. I once watched someone break a rod showing a group how "easy" it is to cast a twelve-inch fly. I have selected fly patterns that the average angler can cast. Growth among some species' young-of-the-year is fast. Just several months after hatching, the juvenile baits of some larger species are of ideal size to match with flies. Certain locations become productive fishing spots as these young baitfish flow out of their protective homes.

There are also numerous incidental foods that gamefish feed on infrequently. Unfortunately, there are not enough pages to include them, and their mention would only defeat the purpose of this book.

The evaluations and insights in this book are those of a fisherman, not a scientist. As a fisherman, I may have misread or misunderstood certain events and technical information. And as there is conflicting information on some foods, and little information on others, cold hard facts were not always available. Add to this the ever-changing environment from year to year and you will see why observation on the ocean is so important; you will learn more about saltwater foods on the water (learning the foods) than you will in the lab. Nature is not set in stone, and being open-minded and adaptable will make you a better angler. This is what makes nature so interesting, and perhaps why a fish takes a fly one day—and will not look at it the next.

This guide is meant to teach the angler to react to a fishing situation; to know what fly to use and how to fish that fly; to know where and how to look and find foods fish feed on. Trying to plan a fishing trip to coincide with a certain event, such as a worm hatch or the time young baitfish will leave an estuary, is difficult. Large inflows of fresh water, changes in weather, and varying temperatures will alter foods in the sea. A bait type might dominate a location one year, and be virtually absent the next. Spawning times and growth rates may change from year to year, and this modification in foods can affect fishing, sometimes drastically. Some baits in saltwater locations can change completely from one year to the next. Yes, in some areas, there will always be mainstay foods, but these foods can move to different locations within an area. Finding and knowing the foods that gamefish are feeding on is vitally important when fishing the sea. Locations devoid of food are generally devoid of gamefish. It is important to locate the bait, then match it with a fly of similar length, body shape, and color.

Note: For those wanting more detailed, scientific information about baits, look at *A Fly Fisher's Guide to Saltwater Naturals and Their Imitations* by George V. Roberts, Jr.

1 | FINDING BAITS

Gamefish in the sea either become successful predators, or perish. They learn quickly how to find food, where the food will be, and what it does to hide or escape. Anglers can learn about baits by studying and observing their habits. In some locations, such as bonefish flats, certain foods are always present, and usually predictable each season. Schooling baits, however, can change from year to year; within a season, they may move around because their environment changes.

Wind and weather are the major factors that move swimming baits. Wind blowing into a landmass will push baitfish against the shore. In estuaries, baits collect along the windward side; look for them in pockets along the shoreline. Wind pushes baits into bowls and holes along a beach. Baits also move with the tide, and at times schools of baits will flow out of an inlet or along a beach, traveling with the tide. As small estuaries drain, baits must leave or be trapped in small tidal pools.

Estuaries are perhaps the single most important locations for many saltwater foods. The mouths of estuaries will hold many foods. Bays, harbors, and any small, sheltered, marshy locations are all parts of the estuary system. Saltwater marshes are the spawning areas, nurseries, and homes for vast numbers of ocean species. Coastlines devoid of estuaries lack the numbers and variety of sea creatures found along a marsh-rich coast. The East and Gulf Coasts, with their countless marshes, offer much better inshore fishing than some sections of the Pacific Coast. Yes, the West Coast has great deep-water fishing right near shore, but the southern locations

Look for bait along a jetty, particularly at the mouths of estuaries.

along the West Coast lack the fish life found in areas with estuaries. The estuary is the best place to study baits. It is a location that holds life all season long.

Herring, menhaden, alewives, mullet, shad, anchovies, shrimp, crabs, worms, silversides, smelt, and sand eels are part of a long list of foods that live or develop in estuaries. In the spring and early summer, shrimp, crabs, and worms are active. Baitfish are active all season long, but late summer to fall is the time when most young and adult baitfish move into open water; it is also a major feeding time for gamefish.

Look around the mouth of an estuary, along the marsh banks, and in the shallows for foods. The entrances of small creeks on an outflowing tide will always have baits, as will the jetties at outlets—you will be shocked at the number and variety of foods holding along the rocky structure of an estuary. Big river systems, like those of Maine, Georgia, Florida, and the Gulf Coast, are vast ecosystems rich with food, as are the big systems in the Pacific Northwest. The Florida Everglades, Chesapeake Bay, and the huge connecting waters from Puget Sound to the Strait of Georgia are tremendous systems that provide life not just for their immediate areas, but for miles of coastline around them.

Wide-open beaches will at times hold heavy concentrations of foods. Smelt, silversides, sardines, sand eels, and herring, as well as other foods such as crabs, hold along sand or gravel beaches, in the surf line, and just outside the surf. Beaches with structure hold crabs and lobsters, as well as baitfish. Even shallow beaches, particularly those near estuaries, hold a host of baits. Many young baitfish grow up in the protected environment of tidal flats.

Very shallow southern flats that attract bonefish and permit, as well as shallows with mangroves, are rich with foods, generally holding numerous crabs and shrimp. Look for holes and cone-shaped mounds that tell you there are foods in the mud. The foods that live on southern flats need flowing water.

Sections of a flat with good tidal flow will have more foods.

If you take a fish home for dinner, check the stomach to see what the fish was eating. Some fish, while struggling at the end of your line, will spit out food. Watch the fish as it

Here the stomach contents of a bluefish show that sand eels were the major bait.

Here are squid that a fish regurgitated. Note that the lifelike squid fly looks better than the real thing.

gets close; it could show what bait it is eating. Fish will also spit up food after you land them, which gives you an opportunity to examine the bait type. Yes, you might be catching fish, but another fly could be even more effective. This will at least allow you to take a close look at the foods the fish are eating.

Sea birds flying over the water or diving into it show that there is food in that location, as do shore birds such as herons stalking a marsh bank. When you see cormorants diving in an area, the location has food, just as swallows over a river tell you there is a hatch of flies. Look for predators other than fish that feed on the same foods that gamefish eat.

One summer my wife and I walked a Maine beach at low tide. It was over three miles long, and one section, for perhaps 200 yards, was covered with herring gulls, apparently feeding on something. Several gulls would race to one spot, picking at the ground. As we drew near, a sand eel popped out of the sand and a gull pounced on the helpless baitfish. There were many birds and the sand was well tracked. It was obvious from the activity that this section of beach held a heavy concentration of baitfish. The three- to four-inch baits were hiding in the sand, waiting for the rising tide. I marked the spot and fished it the following morning, when water covered that section of beach. The gamefish also found the baitfish, readily taking any thin pattern at first light.

Large numbers of birds along a beach whether feeding on bait or just sitting could alert the angler to a food source.

Although there were no gulls in sight that morning, birds had helped me find fish.

Sandbars where birds roost are locations that attract baitfish on incoming tides. At low tide the birds leave their droppings, which are high in nutrients, on exposed bars. As the bars cover, the baitfish, attracted by the droppings, move in to feed, and the gamefish are right behind them. Captain Larry Kennedy of St. Simons, Georgia, marks the locations where pelicans and other sea birds roost, and fishes them on an incoming tide.

A slick will form over heavy concentrations of baitfish. On a wind-chopped surface a slick looks like a flat, smooth, pale blue blob. The water in the slick will appear less choppy than

Look for a slick, calm oily looking patch on the water's surface. It's presence indicates baitfish.

the surrounding water, sometimes almost calm. On calm water, a slick looks oily. Big, oily baits, such as menhaden, herring, and sardines create heavy slicks, but even small baits form slicks. Look for calm, oily sections along a jetty or beach, or in open water. Small round slicks usually mean that gamefish are feeding on baits. You can see a slick from a long distance when a light to moderate wind chops the water's surface.

Bait activity is sometimes very obvious. Look for movement on the water's surface. Menhaden will ripple the surface. Even in choppy water, a sharp eye can detect these baits when they swim on top. At times tightly packed schools of baitfish will rush up, swelling above the surface. In calm water small baits like sand eels show up well. A morning walk along a beach will reveal some of the foods holding there, but plan to be early on these walks, as the sea birds will quickly clean up such easy meals. While fishing, keep looking along the shoreline, especially at night, as baitfish might wash up on the beach.

The way a gamefish feeds sometimes gives a clue to the food type it is consuming. Weakfish make popping sounds when feeding on surface-floating shrimp, and on a calm night this sound will carry for some distance. Fish with their tails up and heads down are grubbing the bottom. In cold northern waters the bait could be sand eels, shrimp, or crabs; in southern waters it will be crabs or shrimp. Fish finning slowly on the surface are feeding on tiny foods. Very small baitfish, baby crabs, shrimp, or swarming worms are the likely food source. Some of these foods are less than an inch long, so you must

Look for baitfish along a shoreline. Not only will finding food along the beach tell the angler what bait is present but here you can tell that a toothy fish fed upon the food.

The way fish feed can tell the angler what bait they are feeding on. Subtle feeding means small immobile baits or baits holding near the surface, fast aggressive feeding means fast moving baits.

look closely to identify the baits. Schools of fast-feeding fish are usually taking small baitfish, as are fish that continually thrash the surface. You will often see the baitfish showering into the air as they try to escape. Loud, noisy surface splashes mean fish are chasing fast-moving baits; quiet swirls mean fish feeding on slow-moving or drifting baits. Here you may not know the food source, but this will at least help you to determine the proper retrieve.

Remember the colors of foods will change from one location to the next. Like gamefish, saltwater foods blend in well with their environment. Over a light bottom baitfish become very subtle, while over a dark bottom they will have more color. Like chameleons, they can change shades quickly when moving from light to dark backgrounds. Crustaceans must blend into the background; otherwise they would become easy targets for gamefish. This is why I feel general shades of color on a fly work better, most of the time, than precise matches; the foods keep changing color to blend in with their surroundings.

2 | THE MAJOR FOODS

y first encounter with sand eels was bewildering; there were breaking gamefish everywhere, but they were impossible to catch. I was young then, and would cast wildly into the feeding fish, hoping for a strike. I remember other anglers making light of my enthusiasm. The spin fishermen would walk away, or just watch. "You can't catch fish feeding in thick sand eels," they would heckle. It was perhaps this goading that helped me develop a sand eel pattern over thirty years ago, and helped me crack the riddle of catching fish when baitfish congregate in thick schools. Many anglers, even early fly rodders, gave up or lost hope when fish were feeding on thick schools of these tiny baits. It was frustrating; even at times disheartening. Here were all these fish, some so close you could hit them with the rod tip, but they would not take. But that was in the early days, the days before the evolution of northeastern fly fishing, before people believed that fly fishing would develop to today's standards. Now the fly rodder, with modern techniques, can often outfish those using other means when fish are feeding on small foods, or when they are feeding on heavy concentrations of baits. Finding a way to catch fish in thick schools of sand eels is certainly one reason why I became a serious fly rodder.

SAND LANCE—*Ammodytidae*

Sand eel, candlefish

Pacific—*Ammodytes hexapterus*
American—*Ammodytes americanus*
Northern—*Ammodytes dubius*

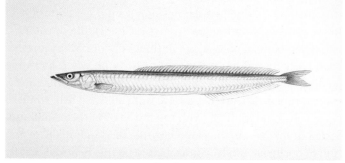

Sand eel

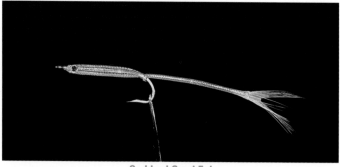

Goddard Sand Eel

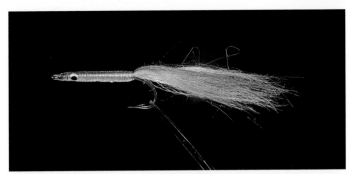

Eric's Sand Eel

Floating Sand Eel

Snake Fly

The common names for a sand lance are sand eel and Atlantic sand eel; sand lance is seldom used. The northern sand lance is an offshore species, and much less significant as a fly rodder's bait. As it is similar to the Atlantic sand eel, all sand eel references will be to the American sand lance. The Pacific and Atlantic sand lance are similar species. Some researchers contend that they are the same species.

Sand eels become important as baitfish upon reaching two inches in length. Some grow to eight inches, but most fly patterns range from two to five inches long.

Sand eels are long, thin, pencil-shaped fish with varying colors. Their backs are olive, brown, or bluish green, sometimes an iridescent steel blue, with the lower side and bottom ranging from silver to dull white. Yellow and green are good colors for flies.

You will find sand eels in many inshore locations, ranging out into the open ocean. They hold along sandy, sheltered beaches, in estuaries, and along ocean beaches with heavy surf. In the Atlantic from New Jersey to upper Maine they are a major food source throughout the season. In the Pacific they are called candlefish in some locations, and range from Alaska to southern California.

Young sand eels appear in the spring and begin to grow— by fall there is an assortment of sizes. In estuaries, I have seen them in schools containing individual fish from three to six inches in length. In the spring, some schools hold fish that are similar in size; in the fall they may mix together before moving offshore.

Sand eels move most of their body when swimming, wiggling like a snake. Flies that breathe and have plenty of tail action are ideal patterns to match a sand eel. Yet fly patterns with little tail action will still catch fish; the basic silhouette of the fly, long and thin, is the most important consideration.

Sand eels will sometimes remain motionless, holding in the current. Here is where gamefish can easily feed on them, and will take a fly very well. But when the sand eels form tightly packed schools, catching can be difficult. In a tight formation, they are difficult to feed on, because the gamefish cannot pick out a target in the thick school—a defense strategy for many baitfish. When this happens, the gamefish will charge into the school of sand eels, striking groups of baits rather than individuals.

Fish feeding this way on thick schools of sand eels can be hard to take. If fish are busting on the surface and not taking your fly, try fishing below the heavy concentrations of baits

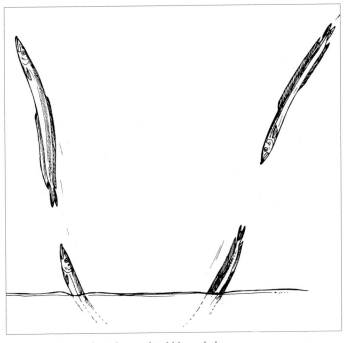

Sand eels burrow into the sand to hide and sleep.

with a sinking fly or a sinking line. Gamefish hold below the schools of baitfish, feeding on the dead and crippled baits. In shallow water, try fishing to the sides of the feeding fish. In both cases you are avoiding the heavy concentrations of baits so a fish might single out your offering, rather than just striking at the bunches of baits in the school. Getting below the baits is the more effective technique.

As darkness falls, sand eels burrow into the sand, coming out again at first light. Sometimes they do remain in the sand all day. You can find sand eels by stomping your feet along a sandy bottom; they will pop out, sometimes jumping into the air. As you walk, keep looking at the bottom; the sand eels will move as your feet approach. If there are large numbers of baitfish in one location, gamefish will visit that area. Sand eels, once out of the sand, will form tight schools, sometimes literally covering the bottom.

When fish are feeding on single baitfish, a slow, darting retrieve works well. Try drifting the fly in a fast current while twitching the rod tip. In the daytime I prefer a faster-moving fly. When fishing below thick schools of sand eels let the fly drift and settle down beneath the main body of baits, like a dead or crippled baitfish.

My first sand eel fly was basic and ugly, with brown bucktail for the tail and gray yarn for the body. I coated the body with five-minute epoxy to make it sink. Today, fly tyers are using the abundance of new materials to create superior patterns, like Goddard's Sand Eel, or Eric Peterson's Sand Eel, and his Floating Sand Eel. The floating fly works great on a calm night when fish are finicky. The Snake Fly and Deceiver, tied sparsely, also work well, and both have a good wiggling action. Many of the sparsely tied epoxy flies work well. Make the flies all white, black, green, yellow, or a mixture of several colors. The epoxy, blended with white, olive, and violet, with some flash, gives the fly a lifelike appearance.

NEEDLEFISH—*Belonidae*

Needlegar

Needlefish range from Maine to Central America, but are most common in southern locations. Gamefish do feed on needlefish up north, but they are not as important a food source as in the tropics. In the Florida Keys, the Bahamas, and other shallow-water locations, needlefish are a common baitfish—barracuda are particularly fond of needlefish. Called needlegar in the Gulf, they are a food of some importance for redfish

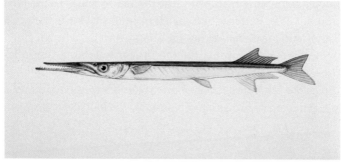

Needlefish

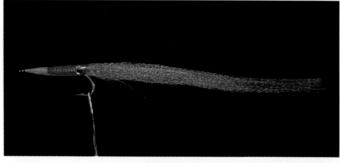

Cuda Candy

and spotted seatrout in the shallows. They are an incidental food in the Pacific.

There are several species of needlefish; some adults grow to two feet long. The smaller baits, ten inches or less, are a good size to copy with a fly. Tie the fly long and thin, with a pointed beak. Bright green or orange are the best colors. Needlefish live on the surface, their blue to green backs and silvery undersides helping them blend into their environment. They swim very fast and skip along the surface at a surprising rate.

You will find needlefish along the edges of shallow flats, on deeper flats, around coral outcroppings, and along the mangroves. They generally travel in groups or small schools, their bodies remaining rigid, with just the tail moving. There are a number of fly patterns that match needlefish. One is the Cuda Candy, but any seven- to ten-inch-long, thin fly in bright green or orange will work. You cannot retrieve a fly as fast as a needlefish moves. If a fish follows but does not take, try sweeping the rod as the fish approaches, or use a slow retrieve. Sometimes a slow-moving fly brings action; possibly the bait looks disabled.

Mid-Bodied Baitfish

SILVERSIDES—*Atherinidae*

Shiner, whitebait, spearing, glass minnow

Reef—*Hypoatherina harringtonensis*
Hardhead—*Atherinomorus stipes*
Tidewater—*Menidia peninsulae*
Atlantic—*Menidia menidia*
Topsmelt—*Atherinops affinis*
Jacksmelt—*Atherinopsis californiensis*
California grunion—*Leuresthes tenuis*

Silversides are a major baitfish in the Atlantic, ranging from the Gulf of St. Lawrence, along the East Coast, through the Bahamas and the Caribbean, along the Gulf Coast, and down into Central

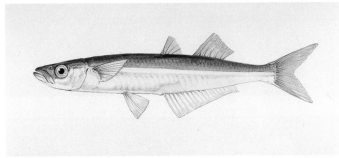

Silverside

Deceiver

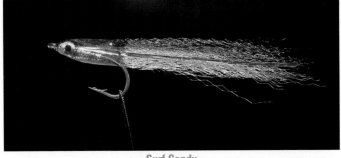

Surf Candy

Skipping Bug

Hairbug

America. The four important species of silversides in the Atlantic are the reef, hardhead, tidewater, and Atlantic. In the Pacific, the topsmelt, jacksmelt, and California grunion are important foods, ranging from Vancouver Island, Canada to Baja, Mexico.

Adult silversides average from two to ten inches long; the Atlantic and tidewater silversides grow to six inches, averaging three to five inches long. The topsmelt and jacksmelt are the largest silversides; some grow to sixteen inches.

Silversides and smelt look alike; both are mid-bodied bait-fish. A five-inch-long fish would be perhaps one-half to five-eighths inches in body depth, with a light greenish back, a white underside, and a silver stripe along its side. At times this stripe gives it a flashy appearance.

Silversides hold in many locations along shorelines, in bays, at the mouths of inlets, on shallow flats, and along structures like jetties, particularly those at the mouths of estuaries. The reef and hardhead species can be found around offshore weed lines. Grunion move onto beaches at night, several days after full and new moons, to spawn in the spring and summer.

Silversides hold themselves suspended in the water. They swim with a flick of the tail, moving with a bolting, erratic action. When chased by gamefish they greyhound, jumping along the water's surface. At night a light will cause this response; do not shine a light in fishing locations. Silversides will, when undisturbed, play by jumping over objects in the water, such as a floating fly line. This is not a good sign when you are retrieving; if the baitfish are hopping over your line, it is because they have little to fear.

Silversides will spread out along an open beach in quiet water. This gives gamefish easy targets for feeding. In currents, or in other locations with moving water, they will sometimes pack into tight schools for protection.

There are many silversides attractor patterns—two I like are the Deceiver and Snake Fly, tied in all white, black, yellow, or hot green. For realistic flies Popovics' Surf Candy is an ideal pattern. Blend green, blue, and smoke or yellow over white, and add some glitter, such as Flashabou or Krystal Flash, to create a realistic fly. Epoxy flies are better with several colors blended for a precise imitation. I use fly patterns two to six inches long, making the flies mid-bodied, five-eighths to three-quarters of an inch wide for a five- to six-inch-long fly.

For fly action use a pulsating retrieve, with six- to twelve-inch strips. To make the fly pulsate, either shake the rod tip or make short, jerky pulls with your retrieving hand. In fast water, let the fly flow with the current, pulsating, without actually retrieving it. In slower water, a smooth, gliding retrieve works well with a fly just below the surface, or with a slider worked on the surface. At times in calm water, flies that leave a surface wake will bring action when others will not.

Silversides are important baitfish in the Atlantic, Gulf, Caribbean, and Pacific areas, with a host of fish feeding on them. They are certainly one of the major foods of inshore species in New England and the Mid-Atlantic region. In the Gulf and in the Florida Keys, 1½- to 2½-inch-long silversides, called glass minnows, are a good food source, despite their small size.

SMELT —*Osmeridae*

Candlefish, whitebait

ATLANTIC AND PACIFIC SMELT
Rainbow—*Osmerus mordax*
Capelin—*Mallotus villosus*

PACIFIC SMELT ONLY
Night—*Spirinchus starksi*
Eulachon—*Thaleichthys pacificus*
Surf—*Hypomesus pretiosus*

Smelt are three to ten inches long, and have a silvery white body with a green or blue back. Any silversides pattern will also work for smelt; use flies from three to six inches long. Smelt range in the Pacific from northern Alaska to southern California, and in the Atlantic from New York to Canada.

Called candlefish or whitebait, smelt and silversides are often confused. (Candlefish is also a common name for the Pacific sand eel.) Many species require a scientist to tell them apart. Smelt are coldwater baits, so the northern areas of the Atlantic, above Cape Cod, hold the best smelt populations.

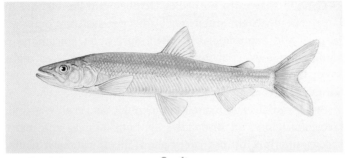
Smelt

Stoll's Mylar Candlefish

Fall and late spring to early summer are the peak periods. You will find smelt in many silversides locations. Because of their likeness to silversides, many saltwater anglers never realize that they are trying to match a smelt, and it really doesn't matter as long as you match the food's appearance. In the Northeast smelt are not as significant as other gamefish foods.

In the Pacific, however, smelt are an important food source. They move into shallow water to spawn along sandy and coarse beaches, as well as inside estuaries; some spawn in fresh water. They frequent surf lines, jetties, bays, and inlets, sometimes in big schools. Salmon and sea-run trout forage on smelt.

Capelin spawn from April to October, coming inshore in large schools. Night smelt move into the surf line between January and September to spawn. Surf smelt are common along shorelines, spawning in the same locations as night smelt, but in daylight, spawning throughout the year. In Puget Sound, surf smelt make runs into the inner waters.

Smelt and silversides not only look alike, but act alike as well. (See information on silversides.) As both families and many species intermix, do not worry about identification. A white, mid-bodied fly with some flash and close to the right length will take fish. Richard Stoll's Mylar Candlefish is a good, precise West Coast smelt pattern as well as a good sand eel fly; but any silversides pattern will also work well for matching smelt.

SARDINE —*Clupeidae*

ATLANTIC SPECIES
Spanish—*Sardinella aurita*
Scaled—*Harengula jajuana*

PACIFIC SPECIES
Pacific—*Sardinops sagax*

Sardines are three to ten inches long, with a dark blue-green back, shiny sided, with a violet iridescent tint; some have an orange tint.

Their range is mostly in the tropical waters of the East Coast, from Florida into the Gulf, and on the West Coast from British Columbia to Mexico.

Along the Atlantic coast the sardine is not a major baitfish. In Florida and the Gulf, the scaled sardine is a baitfish of some importance, but in the Pacific the sardine is the major food source. The Pacific sardine, called a pilchard in northern loca-

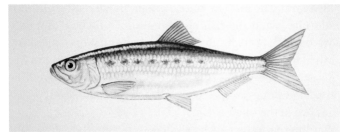

Sardine

Sar-Mul-Mac

Nick's Sardina

tions, is a true sardine. The sardine is a schooling baitfish, roaming open ocean waters. Their only defense is holding in schools; like many open-water schooling baitfish, they have nowhere to hide.

Spawning occurs in open water, mostly off southern California. When the fish are three to five inches long they move back inshore. Adult fish move back offshore, migrating north in the spring and summer, then south in the fall. You will not see sardines in the surf line, but just beyond, where they will hold in some areas all year. Once they become adults, sardines live in the open ocean.

Sardine patterns can be similar to herring-type flies, but should be thinner. Dan Blanton's Sar-Mul-Mac and Nick Curcione's Sardina are two good West Coast patterns. A Deceiver with a blue back over white would also be ideal sardine imitations. A smelt or silversides pattern would also be effective. Work these flies with medium to long strips, making six- to twelve-inch pulls with the retrieving hand. Many West Coast anglers use lead-core fly line with a fast retrieve, starting the retrieve as soon as the fly hits the water. The fast-sinking line causes the fly to dive as it pulsates with the retrieve.

ANCHOVY —*Engraulidae*

Chovy, greeny, pinhead

ATLANTIC SPECIES
Bay—*Anchoa mitchilli*
Striped—*Anchoa hepsetus*

PACIFIC SPECIES
Northern—*Engraulis mordax*
Deepbody—*Anchoa compressa*

Anchovies are two to seven inches long, and look like shiners or small members of the herring family. They are silvery, mid-bodied baitfish with greenish or bluish brown backs. Most

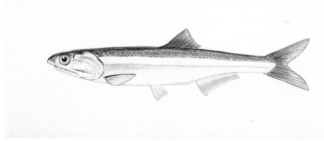

Anchovy

Goddard's Glass Minnow

adult anchovies range in size from about three to five inches long. Gamefish do feed on the young, and some flies should be small—1½ to 2 inches. Cast your fly into the school; if it looks like a diamond stuck in a goat's backside use a smaller fly.

In the Pacific anchovies are called "chovies," or "greenies;" the two- to three-inch-long baitfish are known as "pinheads." The deepbody and the northern are the major Pacific anchovies. They are a primary food source all year long in many locations.

In the Atlantic and Gulf anchovies are a major food source as well, yet few anglers realize they exist, and possibly with good reason. Anchovies look like silversides, hold in the same locations, and in most cases, a silversides imitation works fine

for matching an anchovy. However, there are times when the right fly in a small size will produce excellent results, while another fly will not.

Choose one of the silversides patterns I mentioned, adding a fluorescent green or blue back to the fly. Epoxy flies with these colors blended into the body work well, as will Nick Curcione's Sardina, a popular West Coast anchovy pattern.

I feel the anchovy is a primary source of food for bonito and false albacore feeding around estuaries in New England, and it is also a major food for Pacific bonito, as well as tuna. When bonito are feeding on miniature baitfish, a small epoxy fly will outfish other offerings. Flies of 1½ to 2½ inches long will match the bait precisely. This is one time when I feel that a lifelike match will fool more fish than an attractor pattern. Popovics' Surf Candy and Dennis Goddard's Glass Minnow are two of the many epoxy flies that will match a small anchovy.

There are a number of species of anchovies. Unfortunately, there is little information available about most of them. They range from the Gulf of Maine to Central America, and along the Pacific coast from British Columbia to Baja. I have seen schools of anchovies in and around estuaries, along beaches, and in open waters from early summer to late fall in the Atlantic. They move in tightly packed schools, sometimes flowing like big balloons filled with water. If the schools are bolting or spraying into the air, gamefish are working the schools. The bay anchovy spawns between April and October; some spawning occurs offshore. The young develop in estuaries, moving out as they mature. The mouths of estuaries and along beaches are the best places to find anchovies.

Studies have shown that bay anchovies are a major food source, and in certain years in Long Island Sound they were the predominant food of bluefish. Obviously there are many anchovies in the Atlantic. Perhaps that they are not as visible as spearing and sand eels makes them seem less important; or possibly they are mistaken for other baitfish.

Nick Curcione fishes extensively along the southern California coast. He feels that the "chovies," along with sardines, are the two most important baitfish in his location. Both these baitfish occur offshore, with the anchovy also moving into bays, estuaries, and rivers.

Big Baitfish/Flatsided

ROUND HERRING—*Dussumieriidae*

Pacific round herring—*Etrumeus acuminatus*

HERRING—*Clupeidae*

ATLANTIC SPECIES

Menhaden, pogy, mossbunker, bunker

Alewife—*Alosa pseudoharengus*
Blueback herring—*Alosa aestivalis*
Gulf menhaden—*Brevoortia patronus*
Atlantic herring—*Clupea harengus*
Atlantic menhaden—*Brevoortia tyrannus*

PACIFIC SPECIES

Horse herring
Pacific herring—*Clupea harengus pallasi*
Shiner surfperch—*Cymatogaster aggregata*

Blueback herring

Menhaden

Pacific and Atlantic herring

Enrico's Bunker

Slab Fly

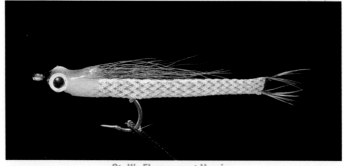

Stoll's Fluorescent Herring

Big baitfish are a thorn in the fly rodder's waders. When game-fish feed on these pieces of meat, fly fishing is tough. Yet, throw out a big swimming plug and your line tightens with an explosion. Without a doubt the fly rodder is at a disadvantage. One morning I fly fished next to several spin fishermen as they hammered big fish feeding on bunker, while I never had a bump. I have had some success when fish were feeding on big baits, but it was through persistence rather than finding a solution to the puzzle. There are big fly patterns that will work; the question is, can you cast that large a fly? Most anglers cannot. The only pattern I would recommend for a fly of over nine inches is Enrico's Menhaden, tied by Enrico Puglisi. He uses Sea Fiber to create a good-looking, castable, large fly. You will not, in the larger sizes, cast this fly ninety feet. But it is the most castable large fly I have used if you use a large-size fly line, 10-weight or larger. The best solution is to avoid fishing locations with big baits if you must make a long cast. One guide I know perfected a bunker fly, hooking a piece of fresh bunker on a fly. The Federation of Fly Fishers and the International Game Fish Association would take a dim view of this form of "fly fishing." If fish are feeding in locations with

Blanton's Whistler

rolling water, you stand some chance, but baits over twelve inches are beyond what most fly rodders can match. However, fly fishing is fantastic when the young of these baits appear.

Alewives range from Newfoundland to South Carolina; blueback herring and Atlantic menhaden range from northern Florida to southern Maine.

Atlantic menhaden, called bunker or pogies, are the largest flat-sided baitfish; some individuals can weigh over three pounds in northern locations. Because the adults range from twelve to eighteen inches, the juveniles are more important to the fly angler. These are silvery white with a deep body from two to five inches long. Menhaden spawn offshore, from December in North Carolina to midsummer in northern areas. The larvae move inshore several months after hatching, most developing in estuaries and other shallow, sheltered locations. In late summer and early fall look for small, car-tire-size schools of baitfish in these areas, In the northern sections, the juveniles leave the estuaries in late summer. This departure is earlier in southern locations.

Alewives, blueback and Atlantic herring, and Atlantic menhaden are the major big flat-sided baitfish of the Atlantic. Atlantic herring are uncommon below New Jersey. They are flat-sided fish, wide in the midsection. In the two- to six-inch range they all have a similar appearance: wide-sided and thin. The young baitfish appear bright white to silver with a blue-green to light blue back.

The Gulf menhaden closely resembles the Atlantic menhaden, and like its cousin it is an important food source for gamefish. They spawn offshore in the Gulf, outside river outflows, and the hatchlings move into the estuaries to develop, leaving their protected homes around September. There are other members of the herring family that move into different locations either to spawn or to grow. Check the estuaries for

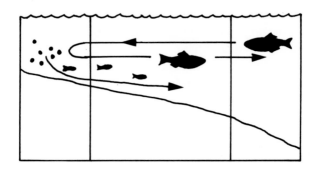

Baits like alewives, Pacific herring and blueback herring move into fresh water in the spring to spawn. The juvenile bait develop in estuaries and start to leave in late summer, some remain until late fall.

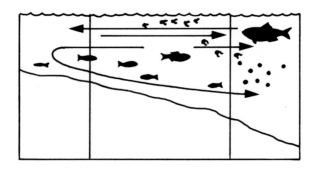

Atlantic herring and menhaden spawn in deep offshore water. The larvae then move into the estuaries, develop and move into open water in mid summer to late fall.

schools of small, flat-sided baits. Bigger areas will have game-fish feeding on the baitfish right inside the estuary. Smaller locations will produce action at the outlet as the baits leave. In the fall, most young baitfish move to open water.

On the West Coast there are Pacific herring, and Pacific round herring. The Pacific and Atlantic herring are closely related; some researchers feel that they are the same fish. However, the Pacific herring, called locally "horse herring" when full size—twelve to sixteen inches long—enters large estuaries and shallow water to spawn from November in southern areas to February and March in Puget Sound. The Atlantic herring moves offshore to spawn. Perhaps the different shorelines cause the fish to behave differently. The gentle sloping of the East Coast bottom contrasts sharply with the plunging bottom off the West Coast. The alewive and blueback herring spawn in the spring in fresh water.

Another flat-sided food in the Pacific is the shiner surfperch; its local name is shiner perch. The shiner perch grows to seven inches, is silvery with light stripes and yellow bars, and ranges from Alaska to Baja. These small gamefish live in shallow locations, and move into brackish water; they provide food for gamefish in bays and estuaries. Dan Blanton considers perch an important food source for stripers in San Francisco Bay and the Delta area. It looks like a panfish. Use a flat-sided or big-bodied fly, three to six inches long. A white fly with yellow barred hackle has a good color mix.

To simplify matters, in many locations these are all simply "herring-type" baits, which provide an ideal food for the fly rodder to copy when the baits are young. Some move into the rivers in the spring and early summer to spawn. Others spawn offshore or near shore from late spring to late summer. In the Atlantic, alewives and blueback herring appear in southern zones in early April; up north they arrive as late as

July. Menhaden appear in early to midsummer. Pacific herring appear inshore from November to May; the juveniles in Puget Sound are one inch long in May, growing to three or four inches by September. They are an ideal size when the salmon move inshore to feed in late summer and early fall. Southern Pacific locations hold young herring earlier. The juveniles are three to four inches long by midsummer. In all cases, the young fish grow up in estuaries or in sheltered waters. The juvenile fish leave the estuaries in the fall, or the following summer. And all these factors can change because of weather. Water-temperature changes, varying amounts of fresh water, and storms can disrupt or alter the spawning of some species. After looking through pages of scientific data, it seems even the researchers don't always know what will come when. There are so many variables. So when *is* the best time to find small, flat-sided baitfish leaving the estuaries? In the Atlantic and Gulf I choose fall as the best time. However, late spring and early summer can be good in some locations. In some southern locations, small menhaden are active in estuaries all winter. In the Pacific, late summer and early fall are key times for small herring to appear. They are a major food source for salmon as they begin their spawning run. Herring in all sizes are an important food throughout the season in the Pacific.

In the spring along the Atlantic shore, big fish follow the adult baitfish, looking for food, and even small creeks will have runs of fish. As the adults are large, duplicating these big foods might frustrate the fly angler. Keep checking the backwaters for signs of baitfish. In some locations, as the baits leave, heading back out to sea, the gamefish lie in ambush. Here you need to fish the largest fly you can throw. Local knowledge, and being on the water often, are very important ways to keep track of the baits' movements.

Is positive baitfish identification important? No. Check size and body width and match them with a fly. Remember, the fish couldn't care less what member of the herring-type family they consume when eating herring, alewives, or bunker; it's all food. If the baitfish are flat-sided and four inches long, the species does not matter, for at a glance many of these foods look alike. We are not talking mayflies here; the fish are taking pieces of meat.

A fly of the general size and shape of the baits will take fish. Flies with flat sides, but narrow in width, are ideal. Make them three to eight inches long, all white with flash, and add a blue or green back to some flies. Blending colors in several layers, or mixing in some pink or lavender on the sides, will work well. All black is also good. An attractor pattern with a wide silhouette will work. Richard Stoll, who fishes Puget Sound, has had great success with lifelike flies for different species of salmon. He fishes them like a crippled bait near thick schools of baitfish, in the same manner as we fish flies under thick sand eels. It amazes me that 3,000 miles away, and with different species, the fishing techniques are similar.

Remember in many locations there are numerous species that look like herring-type baits. Members of the shad family, pilchards, anchovies, and sardines are close in appearance at different stages of their lives, and some river systems will have runs of many different baitfish. This is where learning the foods will help you catch more fish. There are locations that will have outstanding fishing for a period of time because of one bait type. Here you must put in your time and keep looking for foods as they grow or move into an area. In locations that hold herring-type baits, flat-sided flies are a good choice, unless you see other foods.

All these baits stay in tightly packed schools. Herring will hug the shoreline along a steep beach. Look for a dark, moving mass that resembles a shadow. Along deeper beaches with moving water, baits will look like a cloud. Sometimes the water looks smooth where the baits leave a slick. Along shorelines and beaches, or in open water, a slick is a sure sign of baitfish. These characteristics are similar for many of the schooling baits.

Unlike trout feeding on surface flies, gamefish in salt water seldom feed by themselves, and usually feed on groups of baits; the exception is when a bonefish feeds in shallow water on crabs or shrimp. But most saltwater fish feed in groups or schools, and they often try to confuse the baits to make their feeding easier. This is perhaps the major difference between trout fishing with a dry fly and striper fishing a streamer. The dry fly must be close to the natural in size and color, and it must float like a natural to bring a strike. In salt water the fly that acts different from the baits will, at times, attract attention because it appears disabled or is separated from the safety of the school.

When gamefish drive big baits, the baitfish will churn on the surface, sometimes making a loud rushing sound; younger baits will fly into the air when chased. When you see schools of baitfish racing around, there are gamefish attacking them. This is the time to fish your fly below or to the sides of the school, so you are not competing with the concentrations of food. In thick schools of baitfish, a wounded bait attracts attention; gamefish will single out that bait, or fly. Here is where action, along with fly type, will bring more strikes. A buoyant fly combines with a sinking line to create an ideal "crippled" action. The sinking line drags the fly down as you retrieve, and the fly will move toward the surface on the pause. Fished under the school of baits, the fly looks as if it is trying to reach the safety of the school. A short pull, followed by a long pause, works well here. Knowing your fly's action is important, so you can visualize how the fly is working. Herring-type fish are fast swimmers. A quick, darting fly action works best in open water when fish are feeding on scattered baits that are away from the thick schools.

A wide Deceiver, the Tabory Slab Fly, Blanton's Whistler, and Enrico's Bunker Fly are several patterns that have a wide silhouette. A six-inch-long fly should be about two inches wide. If you can cast it, a nine- to ten-inch fly can work when the big baits are present. Or try a big popper. Sometimes a big splash and lots of surface commotion will make the offering look bigger. Here you are selling the sizzle plus the cheese, but minus the hamburger. For a small, precise pattern Richard Stoll's Fluorescent Herring is excellent.

Big, Round-Bodied Baitfish

MULLET —*Mugilidae*

Finger mullet; striped mullet are called black mullet

White or silver—*Mugil curema*
Striped—*Mugil cephalus*

Mullet range in the Atlantic from South America to Cape Cod. I have never seen a big mullet in the northern section. Most are under six inches, which is an ideal size for fly rodders to match. South of New Jersey you will find bigger baits; striped mullet can reach thirty inches, white mullet two feet. The striped mullet is the common mullet up north, as white mullet seldom venture above New Jersey and are most common from Florida south.

Both species of mullet are silvery white with a light blue or green back. The younger, smaller baits, called finger mullet,

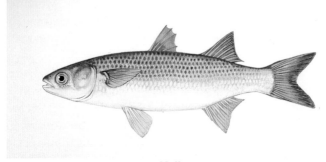

Mullet

are three to six inches long, very bright and silvery, and are the most important to the fly rodder. White mullet are smaller, and in some locations seldom grow bigger than eight inches. Both have a cigar shape in the smaller sizes, developing a wider side and a flatter head as they mature. There are over 100 species of mullet throughout their range. Most are similar in shape and color to the white and striped mullet, which are the two major species.

Mullet, along with menhaden, are the choice of bait fishermen from Virginia to Florida. Watching what the bait fishermen are using can help you find out what the gamefish are feeding on. When fish are on finger mullet, fly fishing is possible, but if fish are feeding on bigger, adult mullet, your chances with a fly decrease.

In the Atlantic and Gulf, striped mullet spawn in the fall, leaving inshore waters to reproduce offshore, returning in about six months' time. The juveniles move into the estuaries to grow, then form large schools in more open water. White mullet spawn in the spring as the water warms, leaving inshore waters to scatter their eggs in deeper water. The larvae move back inshore, develop into fry in estuaries, then, like the striped mullet, form schools and venture back to open water.

Sea Rat

Angus

There is, in some locations, a continuous cycle of small fish; mullet provide an ideal flow of food.

The Pacific has only the striped mullet, which spawns well offshore in the winter. It is not a major food source on the West Coast, and is rare above southern California.

Look for mullet along beaches, or in and around estuaries. They will be found in both small pods and large schools. New England has smaller numbers of mullet than southern areas; expect to see mostly pods of fish. In southern areas and into the Gulf, however, there are large schools of mullet. Along the east coast of Florida from September to November, massive schools of three- to five-inch finger mullet appear along the beaches, running the surf line. When mullet are spraying, or jumping into the air, expect to find gamefish below them. If you find small mullet inside an estuary, keep watching as they grow. Once in the range of four to five inches, mullet holding in these locations move into open water. When they begin to journey out, you could have good fishing. Learning the foods can help you hit a bonanza in some locations. There are several ways to distinguish small mullet from silversides. Mullet have shorter noses, lack the distinctive silver stripe, and have chunkier bodies.

Mullet can swim fast, with a darting action. They do not ball up as tightly as do herring-type fish. They do, however, bunch up when threatened, leaping from the water when pursued. When not disturbed, single mullet will jump straight up into the air. This maneuver tells the angler that mullet are present. Work the fly with a steady six- to twelve-inch retrieve, sometimes trying a pulsating action. In discolored waters, such as off the Georgia coast, use a slower retrieve. In off-color waters, flies tied with deer hair, which push water, are quite effective, because they send out more vibrations than other patterns.

The Sea Rat, Eric Leiser's Angus, and Blanton's Whistler are several good mullet patterns. The flies can be white, brown, gray, or chartreuse, with some flash. If you want, tie in some blue or gray on the back of the lighter flies. Even one of the herring-type patterns would work, as would a spearing pattern. Make the flies two to six inches long.

Mullet are a major food source for gamefish from North Carolina into the Gulf of Mexico. As they are large, like the herring-type bait, mullet are an important food source for bigger fish. To a lesser extent mullet provide food in the Mid-Atlantic area. Although not as abundant in New England, they still are a baitfish of some importance.

MACKEREL—*Scombridae*

Tinker mackerel

Atlantic—*Scomber scombrus*
Pacific or chub—*Scomber japonicus*

Atlantic mackerel range from Canada to North Carolina. Pacific, or chub, mackerel range along both coasts from Canada down into Mexico and Central and South America. Adult Atlantic mackerel grow to about twenty-four inches long, while chub mackerel average eight to fourteen inches. Both species are blue-green along the back with a silvery white underside, and wavy, dark bands along the back. The chub mackerel also has dark spots along its side.

Like the adults, the smaller tinker mackerel have round, cigar-shaped bodies. You will find tinker mackerel at the mouths of estuaries, in schools that range from inshore to miles into the ocean. Mature fish spawn from spring to mid-summer. The larvae grow quickly, approximately two inches in forty days, so by fall they are four to six inches long, an ideal fly-rod-size bait.

Atlantic mackerel

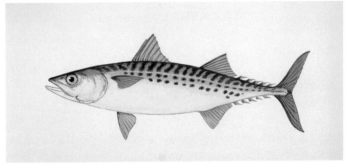

Chub mackerel

Curcione's Big Game Fly

Mackerel swim very fast, appearing rigid in the water, with a fast tail beat. Unlike other baits, which wiggle their bodies to swim, mackerel are like torpedoes with propellers, shooting through the water with quick acceleration. The retrieve should consist of medium to long strips, making the fly glide, not wiggle.

It seems strange that there are few patterns called "mackerel flies," although there are numerous flies with mackerel colors. Many offshore patterns feature blue or green, or a mixture of both colors, with a barred blue or green making the best mackerel imitation. The olive green Deceiver, Curcione's

Big Game Fly, and Blanton's Sar-Mul-Mac are three good mackerel patterns.

Mackerel are important offshore baitfish; yet inshore, runs are not as dependable as other food sources. Near shore, small mackerel become just another baitfish in the food chain, and not the major food that they are offshore. For inshore fishing, a Snake Fly, Deceiver, or Surf Candy in green, four to six inches long, would simulate a tinker mackerel.

SQUID

Opalescent—*Loligo opalescens*
Brief—*Lolliguncula brevis*
Atlantic long-fin—*Loligo pealei*
Short-fin—*Illex illecebrosus*

Squid are a major food source for offshore gamefish, and a part of the food chain for inshore gamesters as well. There are four major species of squid. Opalescent squid grow to about four to seven inches long; these are the calamari, or market squid, found along the Pacific coast. The other three species of squid range from Canada to the West Indies; the brief squid, a small bait three inches long, the Atlantic long-fin, which grows to seventeen inches, and the short-fin, a smaller squid that reaches about twelve inches in length. The short-fin is an important food source in the Northeast.

Squid are round-bodied, and have a cone-shaped tail, with eight arms and two longer tentacles trailing from their heads. The head is located between the arms and body, with large eyes located one third back from the ends of the arms. A squid fly should have the eye placed at the hook's bend.

Squid can change color from white, to brown, to red, to pink, to yellow-gold, and to blue in rapid succession, match-

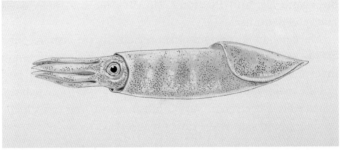

Squid

Shady Lady

ing their background color in the blink of an eye. Squid can swim forward or backward quickly, rolling as they travel, but mostly they travel with their tentacles trailing behind them.

In the spring they migrate inshore to spawn, moving into harbors and near docks, appearing under the lights. They also spawn in deeper water along beaches. Squid are ravenous predators that feed on small baitfish, moving in along shorelines to hunt for food. Expect to find squid anywhere there are small baitfish, from right along a beach to miles offshore; they travel in schools or smaller groups, spreading out when feeding. When squid are around, bigger flies are worth a try, even if fish are feeding on small baits; while the squid are feeding, gamefish will also feed on them.

Squid can hold motionless in the water, slide forward, pause, and then move backward; try giving a pausing action to the fly. Employ both long and short strips, letting the fly glide to a stop. In daylight, for offshore fish, also try a fast, darting action. Flies that breathe make the best squid imitations; even when a squid suspends in the water, its tentacles and fins keep moving. The flies with rigid heads are fine patterns, but I feel those that have movement throughout their entire length are even better.

Fly tyers go to extremes to make precise squid flies, putting fins on the front and tentacles out the back. I believe much of this is wasted on the fish. A Sea Rat or a bulky Deceiver with the eye tied at the hook's bend are good imitations of a squid. One good precise pattern is Bob Popovics' Shady Lady Squid. Make the flies three to six inches long, or eight inches for offshore fishing. White is my first choice for color, but try a blend of light pink and light blue with white, or a blend of light and dark yellow. When using an eye, make sure it's tied well down the hook shank from the head. As the eye is so prominent on many baitfish, adding eyes to the fly is important, particularly for daytime fishing in clear water.

Large Shrimp

LARGE OPEN-WATER SHRIMP—*Penaeidae*

Brown—*Penaeus aztecus*
White—*Penaeus setiferus*
Seabob—*Xiphopeneus kroyeri*

PACIFIC SHRIMP
Coon-stripe—*Pandalus danae*
Bay ghost—*Callianassa californiensis*

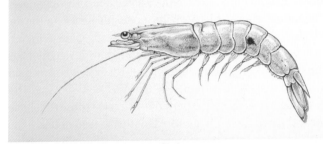

Shrimp

Bend Back

Blonde

Clouser

Apte Fly

From the Mid-Atlantic into the Gulf of Mexico, shrimp provide a major food source for many gamefish. The two most important species, the white shrimp and brown shrimp, both move offshore to spawn. Brown shrimp spawn in the fall. The post-larval shrimp move inshore between January and March, where they grow to a length of three to four inches before moving into open waters. White shrimp spawn from March to April, and the young enter the estuaries between May and June. They grow quickly, reaching six inches by late summer. Some winter over in the estuaries, while others move offshore in late fall. In the Gulf, shrimp are a major food source from April to October. The seabob shrimp, a smaller brown shrimp reaching four inches, appears along Gulf beaches during the winter. Although not as important as white and brown shrimp, in winter large schools of seabob shrimp invade the outer shoreline.

Shrimp in different stages of life provide a constant food source from inside the estuaries to open water. Most shrimp I

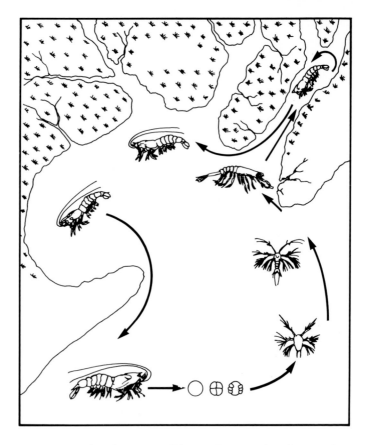

Life cycle of shrimp that spawn offshore—they move into the estuaries and develop then move back into open water.

have viewed in the water lie straight, bending only in flight. Any fly with a "tail kick" will imitate a large shrimp. Flies with flared or splayed tails, like the Stu Apte Tarpon Fly, create a good tail kick. Shrimp vary in color, from grayish brown, to reddish brown, to bluish white. Yellow is also a good color for a shrimp fly. In certain light conditions shrimp appear translucent, with a barred side. This is perhaps why a grizzly or other barred hackle is so effective on tarpon flies. Make flies from 2½ to about 5 inches long, matching the size of shrimp you see in the water. Look for shrimp on muddy or sandy bottoms, and in grassy locations. At certain times of the year, shrimp appear on the surface, floating with the tide.

Plan to find shrimp in all shallow-water locations, from thin flats right out into the ocean. The estuaries are nurseries for shrimp, raising them from winter to late fall; in southern estuaries shrimp are a mainstay. At times shrimp become active at night. In soft bottoms, they will sometimes burrow, but when active, shrimp will swim upward.

When you see shrimp floating near the top, drift the fly along the surface, making it look like a natural. When fishing deep with a sinking line or sinking fly, try lifting the fly from the bottom, then letting it settle back down, to imitate a shrimp working along the bottom. Try a short, jerky retrieve, as shrimp move quickly when alarmed.

There are many precise shrimp patterns. They have eyes, antennae, and tails, and look like you could boil them for a cocktail. In most situations, a basic winged bucktail works as a shrimp pattern. The Blonde is a primitive shrimp pattern. The Bend Back in white, yellow, or blended with a dark top is an ideal basic shrimp pattern, which you can fish in the grass with fewer hangups. Clouser Minnows work well to match shrimp moving along the bottom. White, pink, yellow, and brown are four good colors. Both Bend Backs and Clouser

Minnows imitate baitfish as well. In locations well populated with shrimp, gamefish surely take basic attractor patterns to be shrimp. (See the Southern Shallow-Water Fishing section, page 92.)

Two shrimp of some importance in the Pacific are the coon-stripe and the bay ghost shrimp. The coon-stripe occurs in bays, on eelgrass beds, and in estuaries. They are nearly six inches long, pale red, with blue stripes and spotty white markings. The bay ghost shrimp is found along beaches, as well as in bays and estuaries. It is a burrowing shrimp, 4½ inches long, with a chunky build and a large claw like that of a snapping shrimp. It is whitish, with yellow legs. Coon-stripe and bay ghost shrimp are not nearly as important in the Pacific as the brown and white shrimp are to the southern Atlantic and Gulf coasts.

Crabs

Blue—*Callinectes sapidus*

Blue claw

Mud—*Eurypanopeus depressus*
Common black-fingered mud—*Panopeus herbstii*

Lady—*Ovalipes ocellatus*
Spotted crab, calico crab

Pacific mole—*Emerita analoga*
Atlantic mole—*Emerita talpoida*

Beach bug, sand flea

Blue crab

Mud crab

Mole crab

Lew's Blue Crab

Del Brown's Crab

Curcione's Pacific Beach Bug

From the Mid-Atlantic down to Central America, the blue crab is the most widely distributed large crab. It grows to nine inches across the shell. The blue crab fits its name, sporting a bright blue back and a white underside. Although found along beaches, blue crabs are mostly marsh dwellers. Females drop their eggs at the mouths of estuaries from May to August, and, in southern locations, again in January and February. The larvae, which resemble shrimp, develop quickly, assuming their adult form in about a month. This rapid growth diminishes the blue crab's importance in some locations, because it is "fly-size" for only a short time. However, along the Texas and Louisiana coasts, small blue crabs are numerous from mid-March to the end of April. During this period, they grow from nickel- to half-dollar-size. In these waters they are a favorite food of redfish. Juvenile, midsize, and adult blue crabs fall prey to many species of gamefish from New England to Mexico. The one- to two-inch crabs are the most important to the fly rodder. A crab this size is a favorite food of permit, and to a lesser extent of bonefish. In the Chesapeake Bay, the blue claw is a predominant bait. I would love to have a penny for every crab eaten by a striper. The Lew Jewett Blue Crab Fly matches the young crabs well, and is easy to tie. Attaching some rubber bands for legs gives the fly more action.

There are several species of mud crabs, the flat mud crab and the common black-fingered mud crab being the two most important.

The flat mud crab is three-quarters of an inch wide, grayish olive to olive brown in color, and lives at times on soft bottoms, but mainly over oyster bars. It is a food source for channel bass in the Carolinas and Georgia. It is also found on southern flats. The common black-fingered mud crab and the flat mud crab are both found on shallow southern flats. The common mud crab is 1½ inches wide, and brownish green with dark-tipped claws. They are active in the shallows on a moving tide, hiding as water leaves the flat.

Called the spotted crab, or calico, the lady crab is a shore creature that grows to 3½ inches across the shell. I have found the young of these crabs in stripers, and when baitfish are scarce, these 1 to 2½-inch-wide crabs offer an easy meal. They are present along shorelines, over gravel and mud bottoms, and in estuaries. They are the most widely distributed large crab found along the outer beaches. Look for their shells along shores from Cape Cod to the Gulf of Mexico; they have a yellowish top with reddish purple spots, and a whitish to cream underside. I make flies about 1½ inches wide, with rubber bands for legs. Del Brown's Permit Fly is a good pattern, matching many species of crabs.

Nick Curcione of southern California has had success fishing when a red pelagic crab is active in the summertime. From his area south to Baja, Mexico, this 2 to 3½-inch crab is found in open water, coming to the surface in great numbers. It moves inshore in late spring and early summer. Looking like a short, fat lobster, this red crustacean provides a feasting opportunity for many gamefish species. Nick uses a heavily dressed red or orange Apte-style tarpon fly when these crustaceans appear.

The Pacific mole crab inhabits the open beaches between high and low tide, sometimes in large numbers. The mole crab is also called a beach bug. Pale gray to tannish with whitish appendages, it looks more like a fat-bodied shrimp with a short tail. Found from Alaska to Peru, mole crabs make up ninety percent of the diet for surfperch and corvina. Tie some patterns in all orange, or with an orange tail, as the 1 ⅜-inch-long female crab carries its eggs on its body. To imitate the male, any basic "chubby" tan and white shrimp pattern will work; use weighted eyes if you are fishing in heavy surf. Nick Curcione's Pacific Mole Crab is a good pattern.

The Atlantic mole crab ranges from Cape Cod to Mexico along sand beaches between high and low tide lines. It is commonly called a sand flea. It looks like the Pacific mole crab, but is smaller. Most are just one inch long; however, some individuals do reach two inches in length. You can use the Pacific Mole Crab pattern to match the Atlantic mole crab, too. Striped bass, weakfish, seatrout, and red drum all feed on these small crustaceans, which are present all season long.

Look along shorelines for the shells of crabs. This will help you to determine the local crabs' size and shape. Remember that unless the shell is fresh, the color will be faded.

As with squid and shrimp patterns, fly tyers go to extremes to make precise crab flies. In *Flies for Saltwater* by Stewart and Allen, there are twenty-four crab flies. Some look so realistic you wouldn't want to touch them for fear of being nipped. Pick one, or several, that match the crabs in your area, or your tying skills, or your pocketbook, and see how they fish. Patterns for permit and bonefish should sink fast, falling to the bottom at an angle. This is how crabs escape predators on shallow flats. Flies that imitate swimming crabs—which venture into open water—should be tied with materials that have lots of action, such as spun deer hair, wool, and rubber legs. I make a crab with a tail of flared hackle tips, loosely spun tan deer hair, clipped to a crab's shape, and I glue rubber bands to the bottom with white silicone, for legs—it's so unsightly that I seldom show it to people, but it works. Make some flies with heavy eyes to sink them. Whatever pattern you choose, have confidence in the fly, for even in locations with many species of baitfish, crab flies will take fish. On shallow southern flats crab flies are a mainstay. Yet in other locations they remain a fill-in, a desperation fly, perhaps because we do not fish them often enough. This is certainly true of locations that hold blue crabs, which are extremely abundant at times.

Small Shrimp, Worms, and Other Small Foods

There are a number of tiny foods that even big fish will eat. Some shrimp species are less than one inch long. Young shrimp of larger species, juvenile crabs, and young baitfish are a few of the other small foods available to gamefish. Orvis Saltwater School instructor Pip Winslow has witnessed striped bass of over twenty pounds feeding on shrimp three-eighths of an inch long. I have watched fish feeding on nickel-size crabs and one-inch-long baitfish. These events are not common, but they happen often enough for me to leave room in my fly box for some small flies.

The Hatches

There are several "hatches," as we will call them, that provide significant foods for a limited time. Do not count on such hatches, but enjoy the times when you experience them. The worm hatch, or swarm, is a spawning event like a mayfly hatch. Swarming shrimp and swarming crabs are gatherings of the young of these species as they grow in the spring.

SWARMING WORMS —*Nereis*

Cinder worm, worm hatch

Clam

Palolo

Although called the worm hatch, the swarming of the *Nereis* worm, or clam worm, at new and full moon tides is actually a time of spawning for this species. The worms transform before

Cinder worm

spawning, swarm, then die. The other worm hatch is the spawning of the palolo worm, when sections of the worms break off, swarm, and spawn. These events take place along beaches, in open water, and in estuaries along the Atlantic. The palolo swarm occurs occasionally in northern locations, but it is best known for creating a gamefish feeding binge in southern waters. The worm hatch is an important small food source in the north and Mid-Atlantic. The palolo worm is most important down through the Florida Keys and other warmwater locations.

The worms are red, or red with dark heads; some have white sections as well. The worms are about one to four inches long. The swimming worms, or sections of worms, buzz around in a spiraling motion on an outgoing tide, swimming rapidly at times.

The spawning takes place in spring and into the summer. Wind and bad weather disrupt the swarm; calm, hot nights provide the best opportunities to see the worms. Bigger tides are preferred, and June to early July is the peak period in the Northeast. However, swarming can occur from April to October up and down the coast. Researchers say that swarms occur in September in North Carolina and as early as April at Martha's Vineyard. There is no set spawning cycle such as some baits have, beginning in the south and moving north as the

Paul Dixon's

Orange Blossom

A heavy swarm of spawning Nereis worms.

water warms. In the Florida Keys, the palolo worm swarms in daylight. (See the Southern Shallow Water section, page 92-97)

Most of the worm swarms that I have witnessed were at night, but they can occur at early morning and go on at any time of day. The most consistent times are at the new and full moons, on a high outgoing tide. A few times I have hit a major swarm of worms in Great Bay, New Hampshire, when the worms appeared just before high noon, and swarmed for several hours. The rip where we were anchored came alive with fish, and once we found the right fly, a small red streamer, there was a fish on every cast. The daytime hatches I saw are not as dense as some I have seen at night. When the worms are not thick, fish feed on single targets and the fishing can be fabulous.

In thick swarms, fishing is tough. As in any situation where there is thick bait, try to fish under or to the sides of the heavy concentrations. Fishing a heavily weighted fly that will fall through and under the worms offers the best chance to take fish. A fly heading nose down looks like a swimming worm, because the worms will often swim around on the surface, then spiral from the surface to the bottom and back up again. After viewing a swarm, you will see that the worms flow through the water like a ribbon, and if the worms are scattered, fish will single out your fly. At night, try fishing on the surface with a black muddler–type fly. I use a sparse Snake Fly because it has good action and floats well. Flies made from rabbit fur, ostrich herl, or marabou have a good wiggling action. The spun deer-hair head on the Snake Fly adds more action to the material. Black is a good color for calm, dark nights. Red and white, or red with a dark head, will match the swarming worms' color.

Long Island fly-shop owner Paul Dixon has developed a fly that brings excellent results during worm swarms. The fly is tied with a red marabou tail, Orvis Lite Bright tying material in salmon color for the body, and a green-black Lite Bright head. The Snake Fly and the Orange Blossom are also good patterns to match the swarming worms, for both top-water and sub-surface fishing. Make the flies two to four inches long.

CRAB HATCH

Along the shorelines of New England a crab "hatch" occurs in late spring. The crabs are small, dime- to nickel- size, and silvery gray to brown in color. I have had mixed success with small streamer flies when fishing this hatch. Anglers who match the crab with a lifelike pattern do have some success, but when the crabs are too thick, catching fish is difficult. This occurs in the southern Atlantic and in the Gulf, with several different species of crabs. If you see fish finning, feeding like sipping trout, you are probably experiencing one of many "hatches" that occur in the sea. Examine the water carefully, then match the food with a fly. I keep several small crab flies, plus other diminutive patterns, in the fly box for such occasions. Bill's Epoxy Crab is a good crab hatch fly. When any hatch or swarm of small food occurs, bigger baitfish might be feeding on the tiny baits. Using a larger fly can be effective when the small food is difficult to match.

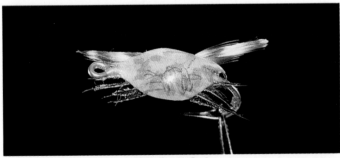

Bill's Epoxy Crab

Small Shrimp
Important in Shallow Water

Common shore—*Palaemontes vulgaris*
Sand—*Crangon septemspinosa*
Banded snapping—*Alpheus armillatus*
Golden mantis—*Pseudosquilla ciliata*

A couple of small shrimp are important in the Northeast: the common shore shrimp, and the sand shrimp. The shore shrimp is less than 2 inches in length; the sand shrimp is about 2 ¼ inches long. In the spring, look for shore shrimp spilling out of the mouth of an estuary, or flowing with the tide

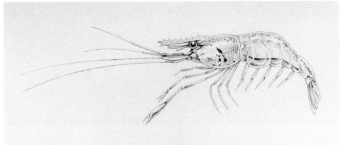

Shore shrimp

Mantis shrimp

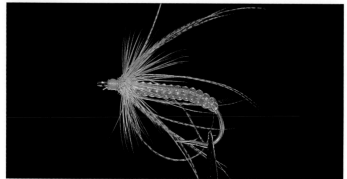

Stoll's Shrimp

Underwing Fly

Dann's See-Thru Shrimp

Mantis Shrimp

Floating Shrimp

on a flat. You will notice that some are clinging to clumps of weed. Weakfish and stripers feed heavily on the shrimp at these times. Sand shrimp inhabit the shallows of bays and estuaries; look for them along the bottom.

Banded snapping shrimp and golden mantis shrimp are just two of many shrimp that live on southern flats. In southern shallow-water locations you will find perhaps several dozen species of shrimp. Many of these species, or their young, are similar in size and color. Yet there are more than eighty shrimp patterns in Lefty Kreh's *Salt Water Fly Patterns,* and many of these patterns employ a concept developed ages ago, namely a body with the wing tied on the underside of the hook. Using this concept, in several sizes, and with just three colors, white, light tan, and brown, you can cover most shrimp, and, for that matter, most bonefishing situations. Mixing in sparse Krystal Flash on some makes for more realistic flies. In many circumstances where you need a small shrimp pattern, this concept works well. Make flies 1 to 1½ inches long. Make some with weighted eyes for deeper water. (See southern flats section for more detail.) For a larger, more precise fly use the Mantis Shrimp fly.

For a small floating shrimp use a spun deer-hair body with a tail, trimming the body to look like a shrimp. I have had success with floating patterns when weakfish were sipping shrimp on the surface. There are numerous small, shrimplike creatures that saltwater gamefish feed on. You do not need a pattern for each one. Good anglers can take many fish on a few patterns; others use many flies to take a few fish.

In Puget Sound, Richard Stoll uses several crustacean patterns for small salmon and sea-run cutthroat trout. They are tied in fluorescent red, pink, and chartreuse. A favorite West Coast pattern, a pure attractor fly, is Stoll's Fluorescent Shrimp.

Offshore Foods

Billfish, tuna, dorado, and other deepwater fish roam the open seas looking for food. Mackerel, squid, sardines, and flying fish, plus numerous other baitfish, provide forage for offshore gamefish. Juvenile dorado are plentiful and grow quickly. Flourishing throughout the warm oceans of the world, young dorado provide food for gamefish. Bright flies tied in combinations of yellow, green, and blue imitate them well. Check the foods already mentioned in the previous section. For billfish, some anglers prefer tandem hooks. Flies should be big and meaty, eight to ten

Bill's Offshore

inches long. A big Deceiver, Curcione's Big Game Fly, Bill Peabody's Offshore Fly, and a popping bug with a one-inch face are all good choices. Blue and white, green and white, red and white, or all white are productive colors offshore. Flies for most offshore species range from four to eight inches long. Sometimes blue-water fish, especially tuna, take small flies, four to five inches long. If fish are busting bait, match that food size with a fly. The Sar-Mul-Mac, Deceiver, Sea Rat, and Sardina, tied in the proper size, are effective offshore patterns.

In September off Block Island and Montauk, draggers haul their trawls of whiting to the surface. As the nets travel to the surface there is spillage, and the tuna follow the hauls up, feeding on the excess fish. Once we had a fantastic day, hooking fish constantly for six hours. The fish would take any fly; I even took one on a popper. Even dapping a fly on the surface brought strikes. Our captain kept the fish hot by throwing out cut pieces of butterfish. That day the fish were not fussy and would hit anything—but this is not always the case.

Whole baitfish or cut pieces can be used for chum, and there are times when gamefish become fussy, taking only what looks and acts like the real thing. If you plan to chum on an offshore venture, carry some flies that look like the chum. Tie a fly that looks like a head or tail section of the baitfish that you will use, weighting some flies to match the chum's sink rate. Although not really a food source, when using ground, frozen chum, the pieces will program the fish into eating. What you are doing is creating a hatch then matching it—a San Juan shuffle that doesn't damage the bottom. Use a Blossom Chum Fly in tan to match the color of the chum.

AMERICAN LOBSTER—*Homarus americanus*

Lobsters are abundant from Canada to Long Island Sound. As adults they are not a major food source, although I have found adult lobsters inside stripers on several occasions. Several anglers I know have experienced a lobster "hatch." They were fishing a fly along the bottom, started taking fish, and found the fish had small lobsters falling from their mouths. When lobsters shed in the summertime, they are vulnerable to predators. Check the fish markets to find when the softshell lobsters begin coming to market. Any three- to four-inch mid-bodied pattern in all black, or red and black, makes a good lobster fly. I do well along rocky areas in Maine with a black Snake Fly or Sea Rat. Certainly, some fish must be taking that

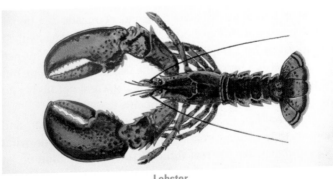

Lobster

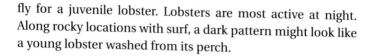

fly for a juvenile lobster. Lobsters are most active at night. Along rocky locations with surf, a dark pattern might look like a young lobster washed from its perch.

AMERICAN EEL—*Anguilla rostrata*

The American eel is a very popular bait for big striped bass. Most bait anglers use an eel twelve to fifteen inches long, but a fly that big would be difficult to cast. Young eels, four to ten inches long, move inshore in the spring. They are an ideal size for the fly rodder to match. They are active at night, hiding in the daytime, and are present throughout the season. Eels are not a schooling bait; they will sometimes congregate, but usually eels are singles. They are a forage species, one that you can expect to find in estuaries, bays, and harbors. Any place with a soft bottom will hold eels. I'm sure that fish take dark baitfish patterns for eels, so any thin, dark, six- to nine-inch pattern makes a good eel fly. Although a favorite striper food, because of their large size eels are not as important to the fly rodder as other foods. When other schooling baits are not present, try fishing a long, thin, dark fly along the bottom. A dark attractor could also simulate any bottom fish.

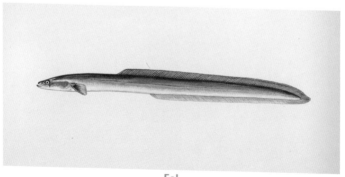

Eel

PLACES

The Atlantic

The Atlantic coast is rich in foods because it boasts miles of estuaries, where big river systems meet the sea. Many baits need such an ecosystem in which to develop. The continental shelf offers relatively shallow waters, in some places extending miles into the ocean. Off the continental shelf, the Gulf Stream's warm waters, laden with food, meet the waters off Canada. Here, water temperatures fluctuate in some locations more than forty degrees from summer to winter. This causes major flows of both baitfish and gamefish. Fishing from shore is perhaps more productive along the Mid-Atlantic and New England coasts than anywhere else in the world. A combination of great gamefish, readily fishable waters, and large concentrations of baitfish makes this possible.

The Gulf Coast

The Gulf Coast is like the Atlantic, offering shallow waters inshore, and many food-rich estuaries. There is less water-temperature fluctuation here than in the Mid- and North Atlantic. With fish active all year, some foods spawn twice, while others develop faster and grow larger. Yet, many species in the menhaden and shad families grow to larger size in colder northern waters. The Gulf has a unique blend of tropical and Mid-Atlantic foods. It lacks only the species found in the coldest northern areas, while offering the benefit of many warmwater baits. At times these foods do move into the Gulf Stream, flowing with the current up to northern

Much of the sea's life spends a portion of its existence in estuaries—both large (left) and small (right).

areas. In the Gulf, the shrimp is perhaps the fly rodder's best friend.

The Pacific

The Pacific and Atlantic coasts are very different. The Pacific has almost no continental shelf; the land plunges into the ocean, with very deep water just several miles offshore. This creates a bigger and more powerful ocean swell. From south of San Francisco to several hundred miles down the Baja peninsula, there are few estuaries. Cold currents keep water temperatures in the mid-fifties, even as far south as Los Angeles. Some locations show little water temperature varia-

tion throughout the year. From Alaska to southern California, there is often little difference in water temperature from summer until mid-fall. Yet, despite the many differences between the Atlantic and Pacific coasts, some baits are the same. There are anchovies, sardines, mackerel, squid, and, along the northern locations, sand eels, herring, and smelt, plus a host of other foods.

Even though the Atlantic, Pacific, and Gulf differ, there are still many similarities among them. Fishing in each location still depends on a mixture of different sizes of schooling baitfish. Some of these, like mullet and herring, live along all three coastlines. Each area boasts several kinds of crustaceans that gamesters eat. From North Carolina down into the Gulf, shrimp are a major food source. Young-of-the-year baitfish, along with juvenile gamefish, provide food in most places.

Baitfish flow in and out of estuaries, inshore and offshore, and up and down the coast. As the food flows, so do the gamefish. There are times when four or five different baitfish inhabit one location, and each provides food for gamefish. The extraordinary thing is that an adventurous angler, willing to sacrifice some fishing days, could fish only a white mid-bodied fly in several different lengths, and perhaps take every gamefish species in all the locations mentioned. The exceptions might be permit, or corvina. However, any fish that feeds on baitfish or shrimp will take a white fly. When you look really closely at saltwater fly fishing, it can be a lot simpler than some anglers make it.

Other than southern shallow-water flats fishing, which I will cover next, some of the fishing in all coastal areas is similar. Flats fishing, however, is a different game. You will find fishing situations in the tropics that are similar to those in many other locations, but sight fishing in skinny warm water requires a different approach.

Southern Shallow-Water Fishing

Fishing shallow southern flats differs greatly from other types of angling. In shallow water, presentation and fly movement are perhaps more important than fly pattern. Performing in classic fashion by casting to a sighted fish, you will generally know at once if your fly selection is correct. With a fly properly presented so as not to spook your quarry, the fish will take, follow, or reject, giving the angler a suggestion in determining the correct pattern. With an immediate refusal, most anglers will try another pattern. In other locations, you would probably continue fishing the fly, simply because the fish's reactions were unseen, or at least not as visible as on a shallow flat. Although there are countless flats flies, several patterns will work in many conditions. Bonefish are opportunists, feeding on many different foods. There are any number of foods on a flat, and a bonefish is not looking for just one thing; it is not programmed, as trout can be during a hatch. But the fly still should imitate a major food source. Snapping shrimp, mantis shrimp, brown shrimp, white shrimp, mud crabs, green reef crabs, cusk, mudworms, and annelid worms are just a few of the foods found on many southern flats.

Shallow-water fishing in the tropics is not as dependent upon, or influenced by, the influx of schooling baits as fishing in other locations. Yes, mullet and menhaden do at times create feeding frenzies, but not to the same extent as in many locations, where schooling baits are quite necessary for good fishing. And some species, such as tarpon, follow schooling baits north as they migrate. Yet most tarpon will hit a fly that looks like a crab or shrimp. Local, resident foods are the mainstays of most southern shallow-water fishing.

Many of the baits on a flat do not move far, thereby providing a consistent food supply throughout the year. There are certain events like the palolo worm swarm, and hatching of different crustaceans, that provide an extraordinary food supply for a short time, but most of the burrowing creatures on a flat seldom change.

Shallow-water fishing is a special game, with special foods that spend much of their lives hidden from view. Shrimp, clams, crabs, and worms are a major portion of some flats gamefish diets. And since this fishing takes place in clear, shallow water you would expect to see the foods easily. However, unless you dig through the bottom at low tide, most foods remain hidden; if they didn't, their lives would be short. At low tide, listen for the sound made by snapping shrimp. This clicking sound will fill the air, telling you these small shrimp inhabit the flat. If you look carefully you might also

The bottom of a southern shallow water flat will tell you if there is abundant life living in the bottom. Note the number of holes and mounds along this food rich flat.

see small crabs moving about. Still, some low-tide foraging is the best way to discover what lives on a flat.

One shallow area I fish in the Bahamas has many funnel-shaped mounds; the bottom is irregular, with soft spots, and many small- to mid-size holes. With gloves I have sifted through the marl; the soft ground is rich with foods, and this location consistently produces bonefish on the incoming tide. If you find an area with mounds and holes, from pencil- to golf-ball-size, check it for foods. A flat is one place that tends to hide its foods, but signs left by the baits tell the angler that the location holds foods and will attract gamefish.

Flats with abundant populations of clams, worms, and

other sedentary foods will draw bonefish. I have never heard of a clam fly, and I don't know—how would you fish it? However, bonefish feeding on such sedentary baits will usually take a shrimp fly. You do not need to match the predominant food; bonefish are opportunists, and eat what is on the table. This does also happen in other locations, with other species of fish, but not with the frequency that it occurs on southern flats. A productive bonefish flat will always have foods. This is not true of most other fishing locations, where it is foods moving into an area that attracts gamefish.

The permit has always been an elusive and challenging foe for the fly rodder, and until recently, most were caught by chance. The permit's favorite food is crab; the most productive crab pattern is Del Brown's Permit Fly. Using his fly, Del has virtually rewritten the book on permit fishing. Choose a fly that resembles Del's imitation, then go find a feeding fish, and drop the fly near it—you might take a permit. The approach is simple enough; if only the catching were equally elementary. However, fly selection for this species is simpler than for most, and a crab fly will take tarpon or bonefish as well.

One special event that takes place in southern shallow-water locations is the palolo worm hatch. In the Florida Keys, the worms appear in May and June as the water warms. The hatches last several days. Researchers say that the swarming takes place around a full or new moon tide, at high outgoing. But Stu Apte, the noted fishing guide and master angler, has witnessed hatches at other times. Stu says his best fishing during the palolo worm hatch was on a quartering moon, on days with low wind, late in the afternoon. He used his orange and yellow Tarpon Fly or a Cockroach pattern with success. Small sections of tail, several inches long, separate from the worm before spawning, then they swarm in large numbers, releasing eggs and sperm. The tiny swarming worms, red to orange, will start a feeding binge that attracts even large tarpon. During a worm swarm fish can become selective. At times, only a precise match of the worm will work. The best fly pattern to fish in a worm hatch is a three-inch-long Orange Blossom; the marabou tail creates an ideal wiggling action.

Remember, a slowly feeding fish will at times examine its prey carefully. Flats fish feed methodically, studying their food. They must be quick, but careful. A.J. McClane says it well in *The Compleat McClane*: "Bonefish are like bird shooters. They spot the fly, determine size, color, and shape and make an instant decision, if things are right." If there is any doubt, the look gets longer and longer. The exception is if there are a number of fish; then competition can take over, and fish may throw caution to the wind.

A good rule of thumb for bonefish flies is to match the color of the flat. Light flat, light flies—dark flat, dark flies. My favorite bonefish fly is made with a tan or lime Krystal Flash body, and a tan or light brown wing. I tie the wing on the underside of the hook and put eyes on some flies. Add a sparse section of lime Krystal Flash to the wings of a few flies, too.

I once followed a fish along a beach in Mexico for a quarter of a mile. I was able to keep walking with the fish as it worked down the shallow beach. The fish moved at a slow pace, and I kept right with it, presenting different flies as I walked. The fish was fussy, refusing some flies while spooking from others. Dark or shiny flies made the fish bolt. As the bottom was very light, I tried a light tan fly. The fish followed several times but would not eat. I waited until the fish turned toward shore with its tail up in a feeding position, then put the fly on the fish's nose. It grabbed the fly without hesitation. This was a time that required combining the right fly with the proper presentation.

My favorite baitfish colors for southern flats fishing are all white, red and white, all black, or black with grizzly. To imitate free-swimming foods, these colors have worked throughout the tropics. This would cover tarpon, snook, barracuda, reef fish, jacks, and other roaming species.

A Basic List of Southern Fly Patterns

When going south, first consult your guide or the camp you plan to visit. If you are going alone, or to a new location, here are some hints that have helped me. For bonefish, a good fly selection should include dark brown, tan, and white tied in the under-wing style. Make some with eyes in sizes #2 to #8. In addition, Captain Frank Catino likes Harry Spear's Mother of Epoxy in tan and brown. The Del Brown crab pattern in #2 and 2/0 is certainly the most popular crab fly. Try the Snake Fly or Sea Rat in black, red and white, and all white, #1 and 2/0; the Apte Tarpon Fly in orange and yellow, black and red, grizzly and yellow, or red and white 1/0 to 3/0; one thin orange pattern to imitate the palolo worm, 1/0; a long green and orange barracuda fly, also 1/0; and some shiny poppers in white, or green and white, 1/0. Using these flies, I could fish with confidence anywhere in the tropics.

Mother of Epoxy

*H*ere is the section for the fly rodder who just wants to go fishing, without researching local foods. With several attractor patterns an angler can fish any location, matching various major foods, without bringing large numbers of flies. There are baitfish found in many different places that look alike. Some are present throughout the season; others appear at different times in different locations. There are two benefits to this. The angler can use an anchovy, herring, or spearing pattern to suggest numerous food types without matching any one bait, or can concentrate on one food that is available in many locations.

MULLET: The striped mullet ranges from Maine into the Gulf of Mexico and all the way to southern California. It is similar in all locations, smaller in colder waters, and most important from North Carolina to Texas. White mullet range throughout the Atlantic, but are most abundant from the Chesapeake Bay into the Gulf. White mullet spawn in the spring; striped mullet spawn in the fall. This maintains an ongoing supply of finger (small) mullet inshore from the Carolinas to the Gulf. A chunky Deceiver, Sea Rat or Angus in white, yellow, and black, or some blended colors, all make good mullet flies. Make flies three to six inches long.

SILVERSIDES AND SMELT: From the Pacific coast of Canada to the Atlantic coast of Canada, you will find one or both of these two- to six-inch-long baitfish. All members of both of these families look alike. In many cases, you would need the research scientist's knowledgeable eye to tell them apart. The Pacific jacksmelt is the largest silversides; the Keys shiner is the smallest. Smelt and silversides mix in the Pacific; both are important foods. Smelt are coldwater fish not found in southern locations. In the north and Mid-Atlantic region silversides are a major food source; the smelt is less significant. Although not a predominant food source in the Gulf and southern Atlantic, silversides still are significant baitfish. A Deceiver, Glass Minnow, Snake Fly, or Surf Candy in white, black, or mixed colors would match either of these baits. Make flies two to six inches long, and add flash to a few of them.

SAND EELS: Although not found in southern waters, the sand eel is still worth mentioning. It is a major food source in the north and Mid-Atlantic, and an important food for salmon and sea-run trout in the Pacific. A thin Deceiver, sparse Snake Fly, or sand eel pattern in white, yellow, black, or white topped with olive, will match a sand eel. Make sand eel flies with a sparse tail and a thin body two to six inches long.

HERRING-TYPE BAITFISH: Herring, shad, menhaden, and alewives are big foods that look alike. Some researchers feel that Atlantic and Pacific herring are the same species. Menhaden, both the Atlantic and Gulf varieties, are major food sources from Maine to the Gulf of Mexico. The different species of herring and shad inhabit the waters of both coasts and the Gulf. Flat-sided flies like the Slab Fly, the Whistler, or Enrico's Adult Bunker three to eight inches long will imitate all but the largest adults. Make these flies all white, all chartreuse, white with a blue top, or a blend of colors, and mix in some flash.

ANCHOVIES AND SARDINES: Both these baitfish are two to eight inches long and silver in color with greenish or bluish backs. In some locations anchovies represent the major food source for a number of gamefish. They are similar to silversides in size and shape, and a three- to six-inch-long silversides or smelt pattern will match these baits. For the smaller sizes, a 1½- to 3-inch-long epoxy fly like the Surf Candy or Goddard's Glass Minnow works best. The sardine resembles a herring. The Sardina, a West Coast pattern, is also an excellent fly. For top-water flies to match any of the above baits check the section on Top Water Flies, page 112.

I have mentioned several fly patterns for each group. This is to give you some guidelines for the basic shape needed for a good match. Some patterns can be made to match most baitfish species by altering the construction. The flies mentioned are not the only flies that will match these baits. Similar patterns—and there are a number of them—will work. White is a good basic color to use. Blend in some green or blue on the backs of these patterns for a more lifelike appearance. For night fishing, or for fishing over dark bottoms, black is a good choice.

The baitfish mentioned provide a porridge of foods for gamefish. Some reside in a given location throughout the season, supplying a constant food source. Most fish are opportunists, striking instinctively, and flies that even vaguely match a food source will often work. Since many baitfish look alike, several attractor patterns will copy a number of different foods. Even so, if you can determine the exact bait type, copying that bait in size, shape, and color will give you the best chance of taking fish.

$\mathcal{S}$ome fish will eat just about anything that gives nourishment—and even things that don't. However, certain fish have a preference for certain foods. Environment and location have a lot to do with the foods that fish consume. Red drum feed heavily on shrimp in the Gulf, but feed primarily on crabs and baitfish along the Outer Banks of North Carolina. From year to year bait types can change; an important food one year might be on a low cycle the next. Certain foods are available for only brief spells. Juvenile baitfish appear for short periods around estuaries, and are the predominant food for a time. But they are not a mainstay as are shrimp in the Gulf, or herring in the Pacific.

I have picked three or four of the top foods for each gamefish species, foods that are present for much of the season. The chosen foods are popular meals and the flies that match these foods are user friendly. A twelve-inch-long menhaden fly is not user friendly. Some fish feed on a wide variety of baits. This is a short list of important foods that fish feed on throughout much of their lives, foods that we can match easily with flies that are fishable. They are not listed in order of importance, because the foods change in different locations.

The list below includes popular fish—it does not contain every species taken on fly.

Offshore fish we can lump into one group: **Tunas, dorado, king mackerel**: Squid, mackerel, and sand eels in the Atlantic; sardines, squid, and mackerel in the Pacific.

BLUEFISH: Sand eels, silversides, anchovies, and small herring-type baitfish.

STRIPED BASS: Sand eels, silversides, juvenile herring-type baitfish, plus shiner perch on the Pacific coast.

WEAKFISH: Silversides, shrimp, and sand eels.

ATLANTIC BONITO AND FALSE ALBACORE: Anchovies, sand eels, silversides.

PACIFIC BONITO: Anchovies ninety percent of the time, and smelt.

RED DRUM: Mullet, shrimp, crabs, and menhaden.

BONEFISH: Shrimp, crabs, and small fry.

LADYFISH: Shrimp and assorted baitfish.

COBIA: Crabs and assorted baitfish.

PERMIT: Crabs, crabs, and crabs.

SPOTTED SEATROUT: Crabs, shrimp, and mullet.

SHARK: Any baitfish.

SALMON AND SEA-RUN TROUT: Smelt, sand eels, herring, and shrimp.

SNOOK: Mullet, shrimp, crabs, and assorted small baitfish.

BARRACUDA: Needlefish, mullet, and assorted reef fish.

JACKS: Assorted baitfish.

SURFPERCH AND CORVINA: Mole crabs ninety percent of the time, and young surfperch.

SPANISH MACKEREL: Anchovies, sand eels, or any small baitfish.

YELLOWTAIL: Squid, anchovies, and mackerel.

TEASED FISH: Billfish, and in most cases amberjack, roosterfish, and cobia are teased up, so they are not really feeding selectively on a bait at the time they take the fly. With teased fish use a large fly or popper. Billfish require the biggest possible offering.

CHUMMED FISH: Tuna, shark, bluefish, amberjack, cobia, wahoo, and jack crevalle are some of the species that come to different forms of chum. Fish drawn around a boat by chum can be very fussy. A chum fly should look and sink like the chum you are using. If using live or dead baitfish, or cut pieces, match your fly to the chum. Give the fly action when using live chum; dead drift the fly if using pieces and dead bait.

6 | JUVENILE GAMEFISH AS FOOD

*Y*oung gamefish often fall prey to their elders. In the fish-eat-fish world of the sea, one does not want to remain small for too long. The spawning, hatching, and developing of many species provides food for a number of gamefish. The food chain in salt water is incredibly brutal, and only the strong survive. Even large gamefish start out small, and until they reach a certain size, they are vulnerable to larger feeding fish. Although not a constant food source, juvenile gamefish in many locations do provide nourishment for a limited time.

Young trout and salmon of various species flow out of Pacific rivers in the spring and early summer. After reaching the sea they move offshore, but when first entering salt water the small fry become a food source. A spearing pattern with a barred wing will imitate small trout and salmon, as they look like smelt with parr marks.

Stripers spawn in the spring, and by midsummer the fry are three to four inches long. As the fry leave the nursery areas and move into open waters the adult fish feed on them. The rivers leading into the Chesapeake, the upper Hudson, and many other locations are breeding grounds. The small stripers are silver and white with light stripes.

Pacific barred surfperch drop their young in rocky areas along the shoreline. In southern California the birth takes place in January and February; farther north it runs as late as June. The small fish are 1½ to 2 inches long. Nick Curcione tells me a small, white Clouser Minnow of this size works well. When young are dropping, the fishing is hot.

Baby bluefish are abundant along the Mid-Atlantic coast. Snapper bluefish, as they are called, are themselves savage feeders. In early to mid-July the three-inch fish appear, growing to over eight inches by early fall. The juvenile bluefish have a herring shape and silvery white sides with a light blue back; they are the most fed-upon baby gamefish I know, a favorite food of many gamefish. Unlike many other species that grow up in protected areas, the snapper blue is roaming at an early age. You will see them up inside estuaries and out in open water. Use a Deceiver or Slab Fly, in white with some flash, and a blue back, or try a blue and white popper when these small gamefish are active.

The young of sea trout are found around grassy flats in midsummer. Young red drum hold around inlets in the spring and summer. Juvenile tarpon are common in rivers and marshes, and are often confused with golden shiners.

Young gamefish are part of the food chain in some locations, offering an easy meal for a time. The adult fish grasp this opportunity, taking advantage of the easy feeding. The watchful angler should seize this occasion as well. Here, the alert researcher who keeps checking the water will strike gold. As with the gamefish, if you find that small window of opportunity, it will pay big dividends.

7 | FLIES AND FLY TYPES

*O*ne major consideration when selecting a fly is its castability: the lighter the fly line, the smaller the fly. Big, bulky flies and wind-resistant poppers need line weight to throw them a decent distance. Casting a big fly is difficult enough with an 11- or 12-weight line, let alone an 8-weight. Choose flies that you can cast comfortably with your outfit.

Will the fly work in the environment you plan to fish? In open water, any pattern will work if it represents a food source. In grassy locations, over mussel bars, or in mangroves, weedless flies work best. The Bend Back, Clouser Minnow, and other inverted flies are ideal for fishing in and around tangles, and for working along the bottom. Captain Frank Catino makes flies with weed guards of wire or mono. He uses weed guards on many patterns even when they unnecessary. Frank feels they do not affect the fly's fishability, and when you do need a weedless fly you do not have to search for it. Their only drawback is that they do not hook fish as well. When casting to snook and tarpon in mangroves, the fly's ability to remain snag-free is sometimes more important than the pattern. Choose flies that suit the water you fish.

In calm, shallow water flies must land quietly. Flies with weighted eyes, epoxy flies, or flies dressed with heavy materials land with a plunk. On a skinny flat, even a fly with bead chain can make too much noise. A fly with a fur or yarn body and a bucktail wing will land like a feather. A good bonefish fly must not only be quiet in calm water, but must settle to the bottom on its back, with the hook point riding up. When fishing larger patterns in the shallows, use flies with palmered hackle bodies or collars, because they will land quietly. A big

Enrico Puglisi's Bunker Fly looks alive in the water.

fly or popping bug with a deer-hair head will settle lightly on the surface. Test your patterns by dropping them into a bathtub. If the fly makes a loud pop or creates large ripples, it is not the right choice for a delicate presentation.

It is important to consider how flies will act in the water. A fly that will have good "breathing" action will move freely if waved through the air. The less a fly moves when waved in the air, the less breathing action it will have. Very stiff flies will have no breathing action.

BASIC FLY COLOR: Sometimes it is better to select fly color for the surroundings and the water conditions, and not worry about matching the bait. All-black flies work well in rolling white water, in discolored water, and at night. In all three cases, black stands out better than lighter shades. Use white flies on bright nights and in daylight in clear water. I use all black and all white in many situations, and red and white down south, but color, or blends of colors, will make a fly come alive. Adding flash to some patterns makes the fly stand out, because most baitfish are shiny. Adding glitter to marabou, bucktail, ostrich herl, and long saddle hackles suggests movement and aids realism even when the fly suspends in the water. Layering color on a wide-sided fly makes it more lifelike, when you need a precise imitation.

BONEFISH FOODS: A fly should, to a degree, match the color of the bottom. Light flats need light flies; on dark flats, fish a darker pattern. Most foods a bonefish eats are dull in color. Yes, they do take bright flies but they probably will take a fly without the flash as long as it is the right color.

The more slowly a fish feeds, the more important fly action and fly design become. A slower-feeding fish generally takes more time to examine the fly. The exceptions to this rule are ocean species like bonito and false albacore. Even though they feed quickly, their keen eyesight in clear water makes fly selection important at times. Fly action, size, shape, and color are also factors in some conditions, because fish can take a better look at the food. Certain species look the fly over carefully. This is not to say that you always need a fly that looks as if it will swim away if the knot slips. However, the basic length and body shape are usually more important than making the fly look alive. There are occasions when a lifelike pattern might be the only fly that will take fish. Blue-water fish, flats fish, and even inshore fish become selective on bluebird days. Clear, calm water and bright light usually require a more lifelike fly. Here is where eyes on a fly make that pattern come alive. In some conditions the eye will stand out like a lightening bolt. If fish are refusing attractor patterns, try a more realistic fly. This is not the norm, but it does occur often enough to make me carry some lifelike flies and small patterns in the box. Remember, there are times when leader size, leader length, or line color are the source of your problem—not the fly.

Top-Water Flies

Top-water attractors differ from subsurface flies because, as they move along the surface, the fish see only a portion of the lure. Many times the splash is what makes the fish take. Poppers are pure attractors; one pattern will work in most situations. The face size determines how much splash the popper will make. A big-faced popper pushes more water, but it is also harder to cast. If you intend to fish a big popper, plan to use a 10-weight or larger fly line.

Poppers work well when prospecting for fish; they make noise and disturb the surface, matching numerous foods in many locations. For most inshore situations one pattern fits all—the Skipping Bug is one of many good popping flies. Two sizes, three and five inches long, in all white, all yellow, red and white, blue and white, or shiny-sided, will work in most situations. In shallow water use small popping bugs. Along the Texas coast, Dave Hayward uses bugs tied on #6 and #8 hooks for trout and redfish. Deer-hair poppers, such as the Hair Bug, work well both as a popper and a slider. For billfish, use eight-inch-long, big-faced poppers. When teasing big fish you need a big splash.

A surface slider is also a good top-water attractor. In calm water it slides on the surface, leaving a wake. Like a popper, the surface slider's body is hardly visible: It is the movement that brings the strike. A foam popper body tied in reverse, with the small end at the hook's eye, will work well. Flies with a spun deer-hair head like the Snake Fly have action and leave a good surface wake. Using active materials in the tail, such as long bucktail, saddle hackle, or ostrich herl, will give the fly more action. Make flies two to six inches long.

Looking at Flies

We usually view flies from the side; this is how they are displayed in books. We also tie flies by looking at them from the side, yet in most cases fish approach a fly from behind, below, or slightly to one side. There are exceptions to this. When schools of fish feed on tightly packed schools of baits, gamefish circle the baits, picking out the individuals separated from the group. Another exception occurs with fish feeding on cripples and chunks that drop below a school of baitfish. This is when the gamefish, circling below the baits, might attack from any angle. If you use a crustacean pattern when flats fishing, fish usually pounce on the fly from above. Still, flats fish do follow flies, and many times will take from the rear. So most flies should look good from a tail view, as well as a side view. This is one reason why the breathing action of a fly provokes strikes, and why flies with a wiggling tail look natural. When viewing a baitfish from behind, you see a roundish shape with a moving tail. I feel that a wiggling action makes fish hit—even when fish are not feeding.

Retrieving to Make the Fly Look Alive

A fly's movement is sometimes more significant than the pattern itself. You can make a fly look alive by using different speeds, different lengths of strip, by altering the time between strips, or just by letting the fly flow in the current. Baitfish move quickly, pause, shoot forward, then spin around in a darting motion; their movements are often erratic. For most baitfish patterns use a stop-and-go action, pausing between strips. Try pulls of different length from three to twelve inches long, while varying speed and time between pauses. This action makes the fly look disabled. Gamefish single out crippled prey because they take less effort to catch. A wounded baitfish fluttering away from the main school triggers the gamefish's feeding instinct. When a fly appears hurt, and moves in a feeble manner, it will attract attention.

A slow retrieve usually works best at night, in fast water, in colder water, and in discolored water. Use a faster retrieve in daylight or in slow-moving water, but be sure to try various retrieves in all situations.

Swimming crabs, like the blue claw, move about freely, are highly mobile, and are faster than crawling crabs. Use a slow to medium speed, stop-and-go retrieve to make the fly pause, and then dart forward like a fleeing crab. Crabs do settle to the bottom, raising their claws to ward off an aggressor. Crawling crabs do the same, but move about slowly, angling quickly to the bottom if chased. On a southern flat, let the fly settle when a fish approaches, then move the fly in short hops along the bottom. Open-water crabs move quickly; use a fast stop-and-go retrieve.

Perhaps the best advice on retrieves is to make the fly part of the environment; make it move with the flow. This is what food does. Watch the foods and work the fly to imitate their movement.

Know How Your Fly Works

It's amazing how many anglers do not know how their flies work. They may take a passing glance as they move it through the water, but few ever take the time to study a fly's action, watching how the fly acts in different water conditions or at different phases of the retrieve. Some flies work better with certain line types. Example: The Slab Fly is designed to fish subsurface with a sinking line. If fishing a Slab Fly with a floating line, tie the fly with weighted eyes to keep the fly from lying on its side.

My favorite patterns work in a variety of situations, but in some conditions a certain retrieve makes the fly come alive. It's knowing how a fly pattern works that makes you a better angler. I believe you should know a few fly patterns well. For the last few years I have fished several patterns in various color schemes, all white and all black, adding red and white for southern fishing. This was for baitfish patterns only, and just an experiment. I took tarpon, snook, bonefish, barracuda, bluefish, striped bass, bluefin and yellowfin tuna, bonito, false albacore, jacks, and a host of reef fish on a Snake Fly, a Slab Fly, and a Sea Rat. Normally I would fish more mixed colors, and add hot green to the list. But I just wanted to see how a few patterns in several color schemes would work. In most cases my success rate was as good as or better than that of other anglers I fished with. Yes, there were cases when a special fly would certainly outperform the flies I used. However, for a good portion of my fishing, a few patterns in several colors performed well.

Saltwater fish eat a variety of foods, and some anglers would have four patterns for each one, while other anglers fish with only four fly patterns. Who would be more successful throughout the season? Probably the best angler. Special flies do work at certain times, and having the right fly on a given day can make that day successful. However, special flies are just that: special. They may work for only a few days each season. My advice is to concentrate initially on the major baits and the flies that match them. Learn the few important foods, the meat and potatoes, first, then work on short-term baits, leaving the special foods for last. Having flies for the worm hatch in the Northeast is fine, but first study the silversides and the sand eel. Along the southern California coast, being prepared for the swarming of pelagic red crabs is great, but your main focus should be on the sardine and the anchovy. In trout fishing, we learn the mayfly first, then we refine. It certainly benefits the angler who spends time learning all the foods. If you keep a log, after several years you will see patterns developing. Keep track of water temperature, wind, tide, time of day, water condition, and the basic fishing information for that day. From year to year certain special feeding events can occur close to the same date. The more time you spend studying a given location, the more you will learn about it. Here is where the fun begins for the serious angler, for once you know the basics, you can begin to unlock these unique events. Don't bet the farm on these events occurring every time; just keep them in mind and be ready. It is a special feeling when you do crack a puzzle, when you arrive at a location and find the water full of feeding fish. This is what makes me get up at 2:00 A.M. and drive for several hours to hit a certain piece of water when I feel the conditions are right. It makes fishing interesting. It is perhaps why catching a few fish in difficult conditions is more rewarding than a blitz in which fish are taking every fly that hits the water. Spend some time studying the foods in the locations you fish. It will not only make you a better angler, it will make your sport more enjoyable.

Fly Menus

About the fly menus: The list of materials for each fly is meant only to inform the fly tyer what materials make up the fly, not to teach how a fly is best tied. As some of the listed flies require a seasoned tyer to build them, the novice should look to other sources to learn tying skills. The novice fly tyer should study a good fly-tying book, watch a good video, go to the fishing shows that feature skilled fly tyers and watch first-hand how they make a fly. This is how I learned. Many clubs and fly shops offer good classes on fly tying. *The Book of Fly Patterns* by Eric Leiser, *Saltwater Fly Tying* by Frank Wentink, and *The Orvis Guide to Beginning Fly Tying* by Eric Leiser are good fly-tying books.

Hooks: All hooks are stainless—I fish only barbless flies, and I suggest you do the same; it's safer for the angler, and kinder to the fish.

The first section contains many attractor flies; some patterns could copy several baitfish, plus a few crustaceans. These are the workhorse flies, the ones that do yeoman's duty. By altering the design one pattern can match many different foods.

Attractor Patterns

BROOKS BLONDE—*Joe Brooks*

HOOK: Straight eye, standard length, #2 to 3/0.
TAIL: Bucktail tied at the hook's bend.
BODY: Mylar tinsel tied between tail and wing.
WING: Bucktail tied in just behind eye.
LENGTH: Two to five inches.

Joe Brooks introduced the Blondes in the early 1960s. Tie them in any color or combination of colors you wish. Tie the tail either the same length as or longer than the wing and add flash to either. This simple-to-tie fly keeps catching fish.

APTE TARPON FLY—*Stu Apte—Tied by Dave Beshara*

HOOK: Straight eye, standard length, 1/0 to 4/0.
WING: Tie in, just before the hook's bend, a pair of bright orange saddle hackles, then over them tie two pairs of bright yellow saddle hackles, making the feathers flare out.

COLLAR: Just where the wing ends, wrap two yellow and two orange hackles around the hook shank.
HEAD: Red thread.
LENGTH: Three to four inches.

This pattern will work with any number of color combinations, applying different materials to both tail and collar. It is one of the original tarpon flies, and is still an effective saltwater fly pattern. Many patterns copy this concept.

LEFTY'S DECEIVER —*Lefty Kreh*—*Tied by Eric Peterson*

HOOK: Straight eye, standard length, #6 to 3/0.
BODY: Wrapped Mylar or leave plain.
TAIL: Six to ten white saddles outside of which, along each side, are a few strands of pearl Mylar, Krystal Flash, or Flashabou.
WING/COLLAR: Two bunches of white bucktail, one on top and one on the bottom, extending beyond the hook point.
THROAT: Red Krystal Flash.
LENGTH: Three to eight inches.

This fly, tied in different styles and colors with a variety of materials, will match many baits. It is perhaps the most popular saltwater pattern.

TABORY'S SEA RAT —*Lou Tabory*

HOOK: Straight eye, standard length, #2 to 3/0.
EYE: Tie in pewter-based plastic-coated eyes one-third of the way back from the hook's eye.
TAIL: Tie in the tail near the bend of the hook, using five to seven thin saddle hackles.
WING: About midway between the tail and the eye, tie in a section of marabou. The feather should extend about halfway down the tail.

COLLAR: Between the marabou and the eye, spin in deer body hair to form a collar. Be sure to tie the hair so the tapered ends are pointing backward.

HEAD: Wrap in chenille around the eyes and wind to the hook's eye to make the nose.

COLOR: I use all black, all white, red and white, or all chartreuse. But you can blend any number of colors to come up with many combinations.

LENGTH: Three to five inches.

Head size and hair density influence the fly's buoyancy. If you want a very buoyant fly make a bigger, thicker head. I like this fly to sink slowly.

SNAKE FLY —*Lou Tabory*

HOOK: Straight eye, standard length, #4 to 2/0.

TAIL: Tie on ostrich herl near the bend of the hook. If adding flash, tie either on top or as part of the tail—this is optional.

WING: About midway between the bend and the hook's eye tie in a section of marabou. The feather should extend about halfway down the tail.

HEAD: In front of the marabou make the head by spinning deer body hair onto the hook shank. Remember to put on the first section with the longer hairs facing toward the tail. Trim the head to a bullet shape, but cut it flat under the chin. Leave some of the deer-hair fibers long.

LENGTH: Three to six inches.

Head size and hair density influence the fly's buoyancy. If you want a very buoyant fly make a bigger, thicker head. I make some Snake Flies very buoyant for surface fishing, or so they won't keep hanging on the bottom when fishing a sinking line. To make a worm hatch snake fly, tie a red tail and wing with a black or white head, two to four inches long on a #4 hook.

BLANTON'S WHISTLER—*Dan Blanton*

HOOK: Straight eye, standard length, #2 to 3/0.
WING: Bucktail tied full and two grizzly hackles per side, curving out, one up and the other down as shown.
BODY: Two turns of chenille directly in front of the wing.
COLLAR: Webby hackle, tied full.
EYES: Silver bead chain secured with thread in front of the collar.
LENGTH: Three to five inches.

Dan ties this fly in many colors and combinations of colors; some flies have grizzly added to the wing.

BLANTON'S SAR-MUL-MAC, BLUE MACKEREL—*Dan Blanton*

HOOK: Straight eye, standard length, #1 to 3/0.
THROAT: Long white bucktail.
WING: About ten white hackles, topped with sparse blue bucktail, then chartreuse Krystal Flash. Tie peacock herl over the top. Leave the herl butts, as they will be pulled over the top of the chenille head. On both sides, tie in a single blue grizzly hackle and blue and silver Flashabou.
EYES: Glass, or pewter, yellow with black pupil.
HEAD: A band of red chenille for gills, then white chenille built up around the eyes; bring the peacock herl over the top and tie in at the head.
LENGTH: Four to six inches.

ANGUS—*Eric Leiser*

HOOK: Straight eye, long shank, #1 to 2/0.
TAIL: Four to six saddle hackles tied in near the hook's bend.

BODY: Wind on lead wire for weight, then wind several marabou plumes along the shank, leaving a bare section for the head.

HEAD: Spin on deer body hair to form the head, and trim to a bullet shape.

COLOR: White, black, yellow, red and white, orange and white, blue and white.

LENGTH: Three to five inches.

SARDINA —*Nick Curcione*

HOOK: Straight eye, standard length, #2 to 2/0.

WING: Blend eight to ten light blue and very dark brown hackles together.

COLLAR: A short section of white FisHair surrounding the hook shank.

SIDES: Pearl Flashabou extending back twice the hook's length.

HEAD: Yellow thread, built up to receive eyes.

EYES: Hollow plastic yellow or red eyes secured to the head with epoxy.

LENGTH: Three to five inches.

Needlefish

CUDA CANDY —*Bob Popovics*

HOOK: Straight eye , standard length, #1 to 1/0.

WING: Make wing with silver Flashabou and fluorescent green or orange Ultra Hair—tie in at the hook's eye.

BODY: Pinch the material together and epoxy over the hook shank to form the first body. This first body should be small, with just enough epoxy to hold the body shape.

EYES: Stick-on orange eyes with black pupils.

LATERAL LINE: Green or orange marking pen.

BODY AND HEAD: Apply a second coat of epoxy over the body; this will form the full-size body.

LENGTH: Six to nine inches.

NOTE: Add a final coat of epoxy over the body.

Big Baitfish

ENRICO'S BUNKER —*Enrico Puglisi*

HOOK: Tiemco 800S or Billy Pate Tarpon Hook or Eagle Claw #D67, 1/10 to 3/0.

THREAD: Larva Lace, clear extra fine.

BODY: Tie six to eight strands of Krystal Flash fluorescent pink at the hook's bend and take lengths of Enrico's Sea Fibers and tie over Krystal Flash. Then high-tie sections of Sea Fibers to both top and bottom of the hook shank, blending in the desired colors to copy a bait type. Glue in sections as you tie. You can make flies of different bulk and thickness by varying the amount of material used. Add in some flash as you tie in the hair.

HEAD: Tie in red Krystal Flash for gills and high-tie short sections of Sea Fibers to finish the head, again adding glue. Then glue in eyes—Enrico burns eye sockets with a soldering iron before gluing. Like most fine fly tyers, Enrico is an artist; I could not duplicate the quality of his fly, but mine still looked pretty good in the water. This fly is the best lifelike pattern to match big baits. Make flies from four to ten inches long.

TYING NOTE: Beauty is in the eye of the beholder. My flies would not win a fly-tying contest. However, they look beautiful in the mouth of a big fish.

SLAB FLY —*Lou Tabory*

HOOK: Straight eye, standard length, 2/0 to 4/0.
EYES: Pewter with plastic pupils, tie to the middle of the hook shank.
TAIL WING: Layer several shades of long bucktail along with flash to form the wing of a big fly—shorter flies work better with several sections of marabou. I use a few drops of non-water-soluble Super Glue to hold the wing together after tying.
HEAD: Spin deer hair onto the hook shank, placing the first section behind the fly's eye, and work toward the hook's eye spinning in the hair—a perfect head is unnecessary. Trim the head, making it flat-sided, but leave some flared hair behind the fly's eye for action.
LENGTH: Four to eight inches.

BIG-GAME FLY —*Nick Curcione*

FRONT HOOK: Straight eye, standard length, 6/0 to 8/0.
REAR HOOK: Up eye, Owner SSW 5111-161, 6/0.
NOTE: Install the tandem hook using a loop of 90 pound test Sevenstrand wire—make the wire loop tight by crushing with pliers. Insert the hook into the wire loop, crimp the wire with two A-3 crimps, and run the ends of the wire through the hook's eye. Then fold back and wrap the wire to the hook shank with mono and glue. The rear hook should be at a 45° angle to the front hook, extending to about one inch from the fly's tail.
WING: Tie in bunches of white FisHair, then cover with long white hackles. On top tie in pearlescent blue Flashabou with pearl Krystal Flash on the sides.
HEAD: White tying thread coated with epoxy.
EYES: Solid plastic red with black pupil.
LENGTH: Nine to eleven inches.

BILL'S OFFSHORE FLY —*Bill Peabody*

FRONT HOOK: Straight eye, standard length, 3/0 to 6/0.
REAR HOOK: Same size and type. Install the tandem hook with coated wire, crimping the hook to the wire. Install the hook facing up, leaving the eye an inch or so beyond the bend of the front hook. Anchor to the first hook by running the wire through the hook's eye and folding it back over the hook shank and wrapping the wire to the shank, then gluing the bond.
TAIL: To the tandem hook tie six to ten saddle hackles and some Flashabou, and wrap pearl body braid over the windings.
WING: To the front hook tie bucktail so it covers the tandem hook, blending over the saddle hackles. Add some flash to the front hook as well.
GILLS: Tie short red or orange bucktail to the fly's face.
EYES: Large doll eyes.
LENGTH: Seven to eleven inches.
COLOR: Bill likes to build these flies in both blue and green over white, adding grizzly to some flies.

LIFELIKE PATTERNS
Mid-Bodied Baitfish

MYLAR CANDLEFISH —*Richard Stoll*

HOOK: Straight eye, standard length, #4 to #1.
TAIL/BODY: Flattened pearl Mylar with a badger hackle section glued in as a tail fin. Slip tubing over the hook and slide a section of twenty-five pound fluorescent red Amnesia mono into the center of the Mylar tubing and tie off near the hook's eye.
WING: Mix blue and green bucktail and tie over the body.

EYES: Solid plastic, glued on to a small head just before the eye of the hook.
LENGTH: Two to four inches.

The next fly is similar but has a wider body and a solid head. Both flies are very lifelike, precise, and subtle patterns. Richard Stoll has come up with some interesting, inventive flies.

FLUORESCENT HERRING —*Richard Stoll*

HOOK: Straight eye, standard length, #2 to 2/0.
TAIL/BODY: Flattened fluorescent pearl Everglow with a badger hackle section glued in as a tail fin. Slip tubing over the hook and slide a section of twenty-five pound fluorescent red Amnesia mono into the center of the Mylar tubing, and tie off near the hook's eye.
WING: Mix blue, green, and red bucktail and tie over the body.
EYES: Solid plastic, glued on before forming the head, or use stick-on eyes after forming the head.
HEAD: Form a solid head with Zap-A-Gap misted with Zip-Kicker or epoxy.
LENGTH: Two to four inches.

SURF CANDY —*Bob Popovics*

HOOK: Straight eye, standard length, #2 to 2/0.
WING: Blend several colors of Ultra Hair with some flash to form the tail and body. Pinch material together and epoxy over the hook shank to form the first body. This first body should be small with just enough epoxy to hold the body shape.
EYES: Stick-on prismatic eye with black pupil, or a yellow eye with black pupil.

GILLS: Painted red with a marking pen; use the pen to add other details to the fly.

BODY AND HEAD: Apply a second coat of epoxy over the body; this will form the full-size body.

LENGTH: Two to four inches.

Bob's unique fly tying techniques have revolutionized precise fly patterns.

DENNIS GODDARD'S GLASS MINNOW
—Dennis Goddard

HOOK: Straight eye, long shank, #1 to 1/0.

BODY: Form the body by inserting the hook's eye through the middle of a six-inch section of pearl Mylar tube. Use a dubbing needle to start the hole in the center of the Mylar section, slip the eye through the Mylar, and tie down at the eye. Then draw the Mylar toward the hook's bend and tie down both sections, one to the top, which will become the tail, and one on the bottom of the shank, but leave the middle section free. Color the top of the Mylar tubing with a green marker. Slide a dubbing needle between the shank and the Mylar and lift, leaving a space between hook and Mylar. Do this to both the top and the bottom of the body.

EYES: Place stick-on eyes near the fly's head. Finish the body by applying epoxy mixed with fine glitter and fill the space between the hook shank and the Mylar with epoxy while rotating the fly.

TAIL: After the epoxy hardens, pick apart the Mylar tubing that extends beyond the hook's bend to form the tail.

LENGTH: Two to three inches.

Dennis credits Matt Vinciguerra's Salty Beady Eye for inspiring the development of this fly.

GODDARD'S SAND EEL —*Dennis Goddard*

This fly uses the same technique as Goddard's Glass Minnow, but the tail is different.

HOOK: Straight eye, long shank, #1 to 1/0.

BODY: Form the body by inserting the hook's eye through the middle of a six-inch section of pearl tubular Mylar. Use a dubbing needle to start the hole in the center of the Mylar section, slip the eye through the Mylar, and tie down at the eye. Then draw the Mylar toward the hook's bend and tie down both sections, one to the top, which will become the tail, and one to the bottom of the hook shank. You will cut this Mylar off at the bend. Leave the middle section free, and the tail long, and do not pick it apart. Color the top of the Mylar tubing with a pink marker. Slide a dubbing needle between the hook shank and the Mylar and lift, leaving a space between hook and Mylar, but make the body thin. Do this to both the top and bottom of the body.

EYES: Place stick-on eyes near the fly's head. Finish the body by applying epoxy mixed with fine glitter, and fill the space between the hook shank and the Mylar with epoxy while rotating the fly.

LENGTH: Three to four inches.

TAIL: Insert a section of trimmed saddle hackle for a tail inside the end of the Mylar tubing and fasten with Super Glue.

ERIC'S SAND EEL —*Eric Peterson*

HOOK: Straight eye, long shank, #2 to 2/0.

TAIL: Tie in the length of clear twenty-pound mono at the hook's bend. (Use a razor blade to taper the end of the monofilament; this will make a smoother body.)

WING: Near the hook's eye, tie in sparse white craft fur topped with olive and lavender craft fur. Make this thin. If you like, add several strands of flash.

UNDERBODY: Wind mono over the craft fur, making sure to maintain the color separation.

EYES: Stick-on prismatic eyes, applied near the head.

BODY: Coat with epoxy or clear nail polish.

LENGTH: Two to five inches.

Patterns for Thick Cover

BEND BACK —*Chico Fernandez*

HOOK: Straight eye, long shank, #2 to 3/0, made bend back style.

BODY: Chenille, wool, or Mylar.

WING: Blend with Flashabou, fluorescent Ultra Hair, or buck-tail with several grizzly hackles.

HEAD: Color to match fly color.

EYES: Stick-on plastic yellow eyes epoxyd to the head.

COLOR: Yellow or white, or either topped with green or blue.

LENGTH: 2½ to 5 inches.

CLOUSER'S DEEP MINNOW
—Bob Clouser

HOOK: Straight eye, standard length, #2 to 2/0.

EYES: Lead eyes tied to the top of the hook, painted to match the fly color.

TAILBACK WING: Tie in behind the eye using polar bear, Ultra Hair, bucktail, or marabou.

WINGFRONT: Tie in between the lead eye and the hook's eye, using the same material as for the tail. You can add some pearl Krystal Flash to either wing.

LENGTH: Two to five inches.

You can make this fly in any color or blend of colors.

Squid Pattern

SHADY LADY SQUID —*Bob Popovics*

HOOK: Straight eye, long shank, 1/0 to 4/0.
TENTACLES: Speckle a dozen white hackles with a black marking pen.
EYES: Solid plastic, glass, or stick-on.
MOUTH: Long-fiber pearl crystal chenille wrapped over, around, and in front of the eyes.
NOTE: Tie the tentacles, mouth, and eyes onto a length of hard fifty-pound monofilament and secure to the hook shank with tying thread, then glue.
BODY: Tie on to the front of the hook long-fiber pearl crystal chenille, covered lightly with white wool or Ultra Hair.
LENGTH: Five to eight inches.

Popping Bugs and Surface Flies

LARRY GREEN'S HAIR BUG —*Larry Green*

HOOK: Straight eye, long shank, 1/0 to 3/0.
TAIL: Long bucktail or saddle hackle.
BODY: Spun deer body hair, packed tightly, the entire hook's length. Make body about 1 ⅛ inches in diameter, trimmed to a round shape.
COLOR: White, yellow, red and white, or blue and white.
LENGTH: Three to five inches.

POPPING BUG OR SKIPPING BUG
—Bill Gallasch

HOOK: Straight eye, long shank, kinked, #4 to 3/0.
TAIL: Bucktail or saddle hackle, and add flash to some poppers.
BODY: Cork or foam—both come preshaped, either tapered or straight. Glue or epoxy the body to the hook shank after tying on the tail. Either paint and use as is, or paint and coat with epoxy for a stronger popper. Modern, single-cell foams are strong and do not require coating.

The larger the face, the more splash the popper will make. Build several sizes for different conditions. For a slider, use a tapered popper body, reversing it so the small end faces the hook's eye.
COLOR: White, yellow, silver, blue and white, and red and white.
LENGTH: 2½ to 6 inches.

ERIC'S FLOATING SAND EEL *—Eric Peterson*

HOOK: Straight eye, standard length, #6 to #4.
TAIL: Black craft fur over which is black Krystal Flash or Twinkle, cemented into a slit made in the rear half of the body.
BODY: Section of round, black, closed-cell foam, mounted on the hook.
EYES: Painted silver with black pupils.
LENGTH: Two to three inches.

FLOATING SHRIMP FLY *—Lou Tabory*

HOOK: Stainless steel, #8 to #4.
THREAD: Size A or monocord.
TAIL: Dark gray bucktail.

BODY: Light brown or off white deer body hair, spun on.
TRIM: Clip and taper to form the shape of a shrimp.
LEGS: Leave some deer-hair fibers for legs.
LENGTH: One to two inches.

Crustacean Patterns

MOTHER OF EPOXY —*Harry Spear*
—*Tied by Jay "Fishy" Fullum*

HOOK: Straight eye, standard length, #8 to #2.
TAIL: Bucktail, marabou, fox or rabbit hair, saddle hackle tips; really any material will make a good tail.
EYES: Plastic, burnt mono, or bead eyes. If using a mold, use lead eyes from a No. 1 to a No. 4 shot shell.
BODY: Epoxy is added to the hook shank, rotating the fly to form the body. With mold, add the hook with the tail, put in lead shot, then fill the mold with epoxy and let harden.
COLOR: White, tan, pink, brown, yellow, or a combination of these colors. Try adding a grizzly hackle or some flash to some flies.
LENGTH: 1 to 2½ inches.

DEL BROWN'S PERMIT FLY —*Del Brown*

HOOK: Straight eye, standard length, #1 to 2/0.
TAIL: Pearl Flashabou and six ginger hackle tips, flared.
LEGS: Rubber bands.
BODY: Alternating tan and brown strands of yarn, tied in with bright green thread.
EYES: Lead eyes.
LENGTH: 1 to 1½ inches.

Originally known as Del's Merkin, it is perhaps the best permit pattern ever used. It will also work well to imitate the lady, or calico, crab.

BEACH BUG, OR MOLE CRAB FLY
—Nick Curcione

HOOK: Straight eye, standard length, #4 to 1/0.
EYES: Chromed lead, pewter, or bead chain tied to the top of the shank to keep the hook point up.
BODY: Fluorescent orange chenille with copper braided Poly Flash.
WING: Tie in white FisHair over orange FisHair, or other fine-fiber hair for the wing.
HEAD: Orange thread coated with epoxy.
LENGTH: 1 to 1½ inches.

The orange color imitates the Pacific female mole crab before spawning. Tie the fly in light brown or tan and it would work well for a basic mole crab imitation for both the Atlantic and Pacific mole crabs. This pattern is also a good large, shallow-water shrimp fly.

BLUE CRAB—Lew Jewett

HOOK: Straight eye, standard length, #4 to 1/0.
EYES: Lead for weight tied near the hook's eye.
BOTTOM WING: Mix several each of natural white and dyed yellow mallard flanks; tie so they flare out. Jimmy Nix makes a similar pattern, but adds rubber bands to the shank for legs.
TOP WING: Tie in several male ringneck rump feathers. They are olive and iridescent green with dark and light bars. Use enough to flare out, covering the bottom wing.
LENGTH: 1 to 1½ inches.

Lew developed this fly some years ago. There have been some alterations to the original pattern, but it is still the best blue crab to date. Tied the size of a nickel, without weighted eyes, this pattern will work well for a crab hatch fly.

BILL'S EPOXY CRAB —*Bill Peabody*

HOOK: Straight eye, standard length, #8 to #4.
BODY: Glue a piece of fiber parchment cut to a crab's shell shape to the hook shank. Color the parchment with a water-proof pen, then coat with epoxy to form the body.
FINS AND LEGS: Glue a piece of a saddle hackle from the bottom section, with fuzzy fibers, to one side of the shell.
CLAWS: Glue on the ends of two small hackle feathers to the shell's front, angling them out as claws.
COLOR: Match the color to baits in your waters.
LENGTH: Three-quarters of an inch to 1 ¼ inches.

FLUORESCENT SHRIMP —*Richard Stoll*

HOOK: Straight eye, standard length, #4 to 1/0.
TAIL: Black Krystal Flash. Tie in a small bunch and clip all but two fibers short.
EYES: Black mono, or plastic eyes tied in near the hook's bend.
BODY: Tie fluorescent pink V-rib to the underside of the hook shank for its entire length, then cover with silver Mylar tinsel. Then wrap V-rib over the body, incorporating fluorescent red Amnesia along the side of the body. The red on silver coming through the V-rib makes the fly stand out in the light.
WING: Mix orange and cerise hackle fibers with pearl Krystal Flash tied as a bottom wing.
COLOR: You can mix and make other color combinations.
LENGTH: Body 1 ⅛ inches long, entire fly 3 inches.

DANN JACOBUS' MANTIS SHRIMP
—Dann Jacobus

HOOK: Long shank, #2 to 1/0.
TAIL: Burnt mono.
UNDERBODY: Tan fur.
COLLAR: Tan or brown grizzly saddle hackle.
ABDOMEN: Tan ostrich.
OVERBODY: Tan bucktail with epoxy over.
ANTENNAE: Optional—pearl Krystal Flash.
LENGTH: Two to three inches.

DANN JACOBUS' SEE-THRU SHRIMP
—Dann Jacobus

HOOK: Short or long shank, #4 to #1.
BODY: Mylar, short.
WING: White or light beige craft fur, long.
THORAX: Gray or white ostrich herl.
EYES: Smallest silver bead chain.
ANTENNAE: Pearl Krystal Flash.
LENGTH: 1 to 2½ inches.

UNDER-WING FLY

This pattern uses the basic under-wing concept that many shrimp-type flies employ. There is no limit to the number of patterns that you can spawn from the Frankee-Belle, developed nearly five decades ago.

HOOK: Straight eye, standard length, or make bend back, but not a hard bend—stainless steel #8 to #10.
EYES: Optional—silver bead chain—make some flies with a flared deer-hair head so they land silently.

BODY: Light green or pearl Krystal Flash, wrapped on the hook shank—on some flies leave several long strands to mix with the wing.

WING: Bleach brown deer tail to a tan color and tie near the hook's eye as an inverted wing. I also make this fly in white and dark brown.

LENGTH: One to two inches.

I make three basic styles of this fly—some with eyes, to sink fast, some without eyes for a silent medium sink rate, and some with a flared head for very quiet entry and slow sink. I check all my bonefish flies to be sure that they settle to the bottom in an upright position. I like the fly because it is simple to tie, it settles correctly in the water, and it looks like a variety of shrimp.

Worm Hatch Patterns

PAUL DIXON'S WORM HATCH FLY
—Paul Dixon

HOOK: Straight eye, standard length, #4 to 1/0.
TAIL: Red marabou.
BODY: Salmon pink Lite Bright dubbed onto two-thirds of the hook shank. Green/black Lite Bright dubbed onto the rest of the hook shank.
LENGTH: 2 to 3½ inches.

BLOSSOM

HOOK: Straight eye, standard length, #1 to 2/0.
TAIL: Marabou tied in just before the bend—make full.
BODY: Chenille tied to the hook's eye.
COLOR: Any.

LENGTH: 2½ to 4 inches.

This fly can be a worm hatch fly, or baitfish imitation as well as a chum fly.

Chum Fly

BLOSSOM CHUM FLY

HOOK: Straight eye, standard length, #2 to 2/0.
TAIL: Fully dressed marabou tied halfway up the hook shank.
BODY: Weight some flies with lead wire—make heavy, medium, and nonweighted flies. Cover the remainder of the body with thick chenille.
COLOR: Make flies tan or reddish brown, or white with a streak of red.
LENGTH: Two to three inches.

BIBLIOGRAPHY

Amos, Stephen H. *Familiar Seashore Creatures, The Audubon Society Pocket Guides.* New York: Alfred A. Knopf, Inc., 1990

Amos, William H., and Stephen H. Amos. *The Audubon Society Nature Guides, Atlantic and Gulf Coasts.* New York: Alfred A. Knopf, Inc., 1985

Arnold, Augusta Foote. *The Sea-Beach at Ebb-Tide.* New York: Dover Publications, Inc., n.d.

Bay, Kenneth E. and Hermann Kessler. *Salt Water Flies.* New York: J.B. Lippincott Co., 1972

Berrill, Michael and Deborah. *The North Atlantic Coast: A Sierra Club Naturalist's Guide.* San Francisco: Sierra Club Books, 1981

Bigelow, Henry B., and William C. Schroeder. *Fishes of the Gulf of Maine.* United States Fish and Wildlife Service, Fisheries Bulletin 74, Volume 53, United States Printing Office, 1953

Brooks, Joe. *The Complete Book of Fly Fishing.* New York: Outdoor Life, 1958

Brown, Dick. *Fly Fishing for Bonefish.* New York: Lyons & Burford, 1993

Carson, Rachel. *The Edge of the Sea.* Boston: Houghton Mifflin Co., 1955

Collins, Henry Hill Jr. *Complete Field Guide to American Wildlife.* New York: Harper & Row, Publishers, 1959

Common and Scientific Names of Fishes from the United States and Canada. American Fisheries Society Special Publication 20, Bethesda, MD, 1991

DeLacy, Allen C., Bruce S. Miller, and Steven F. Borton. *Checklist of Puget Sound Fishes.* Seattle: Division of Marine Resources University of Washington, 1972

Emmett, R.L., S.L. Stone, S.A. Hinton, and M.E. Monaco. *Distribution and Abundance of Fishes and Invertebrates in West Coast Estuaries Volume II: Species Life History Summaries.* Rockville, MD: ELMR Rep. No. 8 NOAA/NOS Strategic Environmental Assessments Division, 1991

Eschmeyer, William N., Earl S. Herald, and Howard Hammann. *A Field Guide to Pacific Coast Fishes of North America.* Boston: Houghton Mifflin Co., 1983

Georgia Department of Natural Resources Coastal Resources Division, *Diagram of the Life Cycle of the White Shrimp.*

Goldstein, Robert J. *Coastal Fishing in the Carolinas.* Winston-Salem: John F. Blair, Publisher, 1986

Gosner, Kenneth L. *A Field Guide to the Atlantic Seashore.* Boston: Houghton Mifflin Co., 1978

Hart, J.L. *Pacific Fishes of Canada.* Ottawa: Fisheries Research Board of Canada, 1973

Hoese, H. Dickson, and Richard H. Moore, and V. Farley Sonnier. *Fishes of the Gulf of Mexico.* College Station: Texas A & M University Press, 1977

Kreh, Bernard, "Lefty." *Fly Fishing in Salt Water.* New York: Lyons & Burford, 1984

Salt Water Fly Patterns. Fullerton, CA.: MARAL, n.d.; rev. ed., Lyons & Burford, 1995

Leiser, Eric. *The Book of Fly Patterns.* New York: Alfred A. Knopf, Inc., 1987

Lippson, Alice Jane and Robert L. *Life in the Chesapeake Bay.* Baltimore: The Johns Hopkins University Press, 1984

McClane, A.J. (Editor). *McClane's New Standard Fishing Encyclopedia.* New York: Holt, Rinehart and Winston, Inc., 1965

McClane, A.J. (Editor). *McClane's Field Guide to Salt Water Fishes of North America.* New York: Holt, Rinehart and Winston, Inc., 1965

McClane, A.J. *The Compleat McClane.* New York: E.P. Dutton, 1988

McKenzie, R.A. and L.R. Day. *The Smelt, Capelin and Silverside.* St. Andrews, N.B.: Fisheries Research Board of Canada, Atlantic Biological Station, General Series, No. 15, 1949

Meinkoth, Norman A. *The Audubon Society Field Guide to North American Seashore Creatures.* New York: Alfred A. Knopf, Inc., 1981

Roberts, George V. Jr. *A Fly-Fisher's Guide to Salt Water.* Camden, ME: Ragged Mountain Press, 1994

Robins, C. Richard, G. Carleton Ray, and John Douglass. *A Field Guide to Atlantic Coast Fishes of North America.* Boston: Houghton Mifflin Co., 1986

Ross, Michael R. and Robert C. Biagi. *Marine Recreational Fisheries of Massachusetts, Rainbow Smelt.* Boston University of Massachusetts Cooperative Extension, : n.d.

Stewart, Dick and Farrow Allen. *Flies for Saltwater.* North Conway: Mountain Pond Publishing, 1992

Surette, Dick (Editor). *Fly Tyer's Pattern Bible.* North Conway: Saco River Publishing Corporation, 1985

Tabory, Lou. *Inshore Fly Fishing.* New York: Lyons & Burford, 1992

Thomson, Keith Stewart, W.H. Weed III, and Algis G. Taruski. *Salt Water Fishes of Connecticut.* State Geological and Natural History Survey of Connecticut, Bulletin 105, 1971

United States Department of the Interior Fish and Wildlife Service Species Profiles: Life Histories and Environmental

Requirements of Coastal Fishes and Invertebrates (North Atlantic). 1986

Wentink, Frank. *Saltwater Fly Tying.* New York: Lyons & Burford, 1991

INDEX